70

© 2023 McSweeney's Quarterly Concern and the contributors, San Francisco, California. ASSISTED BY: Claire Boyle, Eliza Browning, Rita Bullwinkel, Justin Carder, Emma-Li Downer, Daniel Gumbiner, Kim Hew-Low, Emily Lang, Stephanie Pierson, Alexander Rothstein, Raj Tawney, and Katherine Williams. WEBSITE: Chris Monks. COPY EDITOR: Caitlin Van Dusen. ASSOCIATE EDITOR: Lucy Huber. DIRECTOR OF SALES AND DISTRIBUTION: Dan Weiss. TECHNOLOGY DIRECTOR: Nikky Southerland. PRODUCTION MANAGER: Annie Dills. ART DIRECTOR: Sunra Thompson. FOUNDING EDITOR: Dave Eggers. EXECUTIVE DIRECTOR: Amanda Uhle. DEPUTY EDITOR: James Yeh.

COVER ILLUSTRATIONS: Bianca Bagnarelli.

INTERIOR ILLUSTRATIONS: Anuj Shrestha.

Printed in the United States.

This project is supported in part by the National Endowment for the Arts. To find out more about how National Endowment for the Arts grants impact individuals and communities, visit www.arts.gov.

NATIONAL ENDOWMENT for the ARTS
arts.gov

DEAR McSWEENEY'S,

Do you ever worry that your capacity for surprise is on the wane? The older I get, the rarer it becomes that I have an experience for which I don't have a preprogrammed script to help me process it, but which I must instead deal with in real time, and by doing so, learn something about myself. Not that I view myself as a computer or anything, but I do sometimes worry that I'm becoming a robot. Which I guess is just a mechanical body with a computer on top, so maybe that's the same thing.

I've been reading Gary Indiana's memoir recently, and he describes his memories of crusting around the early-'80s Los Angeles punk scene as having all "run together, as a long vacation in a country no longer indicated on any map." Of course Gary probably feels that way because of all the drugs he was doing at the time, but we shouldn't discount the narcotic pleasures of comfortable, cyclical boredom, and of nesting in place while watching one's shows and drinking one's wine from a box.

But! I have begun to leave the couch, to sip wine fresh from the cask of the real, and have rediscovered my sense of wonder. I first noticed this at a cottage in Upstate New York where we stayed, whose backyard was home to a small community of chickens and ducks. Did you know that, if faced with a younger peer—even their own offspring—chickens will attempt to peck it to death? (The ducks did not do this, and the chickens did not display similar murderous impulses toward them.) Which is why our Airbnb host had a two-week-old chick living in a Container Store bin in her garage, leaving her in our care for long periods of time, as the rest of the flock cavorted around the backyard.

The baby chicken did not like this—so much so that one evening as we took in the air, she leaped out of her ad hoc pen and began making her way toward the big kids, announcing her presence by cheep-cheep-cheeping under my chair. I thought of the adage, credited to the late Sam Snead, that one should grip a golf club with the same gentle stability with which one might hold a baby bird, and attempted the opposite. She didn't mind being held as much as she resented that her joyride had come to an end. Back in the garage, door safely closed behind us, we gave her handfuls of meal worms as a consolation prize. She ate them out of our hands, and each precise peck felt like a pair of tweezers gently pinching the folds of our skin.

The next morning we went

to check on her, and she greeted us with a flurry of whistles— a chick's way of communicating happiness, Google told us. More meal worms, more little pecks. After returning her to the bin, I ran my finger across the feathers on her back. She purred.

From this, I learned two things: One, that I cannot consume members of a species after I have developed a personal relationship with one of their representatives. And two, that freedom is the natural state of the chicken. Surprises, both of them.

We've lived in Philadelphia for a year and a half now, and I can confidently say that it is not like most places. Pro wrestling seems to be happening always, and it is being done by anarchists and punks and metalheads, seemingly all vegans. On New Year's Day, troupes of costumed drunks march through town in unison, at considerable cost to the city and for no real reason other than because they can, and besides, everybody loves a good parade—or even a bad one, if it's big and enthusiastic enough. A man on my block, a Teamster, once kept his car parked in the same spot for a year because, he claimed, it was too good a spot to give up; how he got to work during that time I have absolutely no idea. Everyone is

friendly and gruff, especially at the bars where you can still smoke indoors, and new residents such as ourselves seem like a drop in the bucket of an unchanging culture. Decades of unions and cheap rents have helped make a preponderance of free time the norm, and the city's largest park is made up mostly of untouched forest. The first time we took our "outside" dog there (our other dog, while lovely, has to stay at home), he navigated the trails leashless, as if he'd always known the way.

One thing that confuses me, though, *McSweeney's*, is that while marijuana is legal here, the keeping of pet chickens for recreational use is not. For the past two years, the local media has grumbled about repealing this statute at the beginning of spotted lantern fly season—chickens love eating bugs—but Philadelphia remains one of two major chicken-less American cities (the other being Detroit, which seems like a significant fact).

All this helps explain how, one Sunday in November, I would have tripped over the baby chicken scrounging in the cracks of the South Philadelphia sidewalk, two blocks from our home, had my partner not alerted me to its presence. The chick that had been so transformational for me seemed to have a bluish tinge and black wings and a white bib, specked with gray all over. This one was golden brown and noticeably plump, chirping with glee as she tugged at a weed growing out of the concrete. (A note: though the archetypal chick is Peeps yellow, they also come in white, brown, red-brown, gray, and black, mixed in countless patterns.) Another thing about Philadelphia is that live-poultry markets, existing in various states of legality, dot the city, and there were two within a half mile of where we stood. It was cold, and this chick, who'd decided to make a run for it in these streets so institutionally opposed to her very presence, wanted to live. I whipped around, noticed a guy at the bus stop, and asked him if he happened to live around here and had a cardboard box to put it in. "No," he said, "but there's another one right next to you." And there it was, hopping up into someone's container garden and setting up shop.

I grabbed a box from our house and gingerly plopped them in. Despite being the same age, they started pecking each other, so I let one out—there was enough soil in that plot of sidewalk to keep her occupied—as my partner doubled back home for a second box. Once

they were safely housed, we called the local animal shelter and asked if they accepted chickens. They did, the person on the line told me, and they would be sent to a farm.

When we got there, I asked a pair of men smoking cigarettes next to an official-looking truck which door we needed to take these chickens through. "Entrance is right around the other side," one said. "Happens all the time." The lobby was populated by a couple employees behind a desk and some volunteers watching over half a dozen freshly rescued cats who were doing their best to collapse into the backs of their crates as their eyes darted around, on guard for threats. They relaxed only after hearing our chickens' scratching in their boxes; the chicks must have sounded delicious. The volunteer ignored our pleas to keep the chicks separated so they wouldn't bicker, and instead deposited them in a single carrier, lined with newspaper, and with water at the ready. I started to wonder if we should've kept them for ourselves, raising them in the backyard surreptitiously and one day bribing our neighbors with their eggs so that they would keep mum. I was a little mystified that these creatures had appeared at all, but mostly, I was nervous. Were these chickens, despite their bravery and compulsion to seek liberty, even physically capable of survival outside a cramped metal cage, being overfed in unsanitary conditions? Or did waiting around to die in a slaughterhouse instead steel their resolve to get the hell out of there the first chance they got?

The chicks seemed peaceful inside their temporary digs, nestling together for warmth. When I stuck my face up to the little plastic window, I swore I heard a purr. Perhaps their ordeal had bonded them, or maybe they'd simply had a misunderstanding the first time they'd shared a confined space. I didn't know what would happen to them, what the "farm" would be like, or if they'd even make it out of the shelter with all those cats around. But if an animal escapes certain death, it should be rewarded with the chance to have a real life. And if we're lucky enough to have such a gift already, we should follow it to see where it takes us.

Sincerely yours,

DREW MILLARD
PHILADELPHIA, PA

DEAR McSWEENEY'S,
The flora here, just outside the barbed-wire boundary of Camp Humphreys, the largest US military base overseas, is crisp and spindly, a mid-fall burnt sienna. Red-orange persimmons dangle from leafless branches, and stubborn reeds grip the mudbanks of Anseong Creek. Inside the base, the plants are young and manicured—disciplined. Our group stares through the fence; we clamp our ears when the sky goes dark with metal. But only H. knows enough to distinguish a Boeing EA-18G Growler from a General Dynamics F-16 Fighting Falcon from a commercial jet whose destination I imagine to be an opposite kind of place: one characterized by silence and by waxy, emerald-green vegetation.

On the walking path that encircles the base, we watch the lines carved by magpies in black-and-sapphire dress and talk too long about a messy pile of animal shit (and who might have done the shitting). L. shows me a small plant believed to have Viagra-like properties, then points out a pair of musk deer who have somehow made it onto the base and are now prostrate on a patch of grass between a runway and an ammunition bunker. I have never seen musk deer, with their comically vampiric fangs and doglike rumps, in anything but a photograph. I wish I had binoculars to verify their presence.

L., H., and the others are walking; always looking and walking. They know the endless fence of this base (United States Army, enormous) and the other base (United States Air Force, very big) across town. How are there two in this tiny city in tiny South Korea? Every Thursday morning, they gather to look for signs of new military construction or the movement of extraordinary arms: bombers, Patriot missiles, radar systems, clusters of tanks. They call themselves monitors or lookouts. Other people call them anti-base activists or, more simply, anti-American.

I tag along to watch them watch for things. Today the skies of Pyeongtaek are noisy and full, as they have been for weeks, during this extended round of international war games. The Americans, the South Koreans, and the Japanese—reluctantly allied—continue to test and show off their bombs, ships, planes, drones, tanks, helicopters, pontoon bridges, submarines, and missile-defense systems. H. catalogs each sighting in a peacenik group chat, in the manner of a cyber-apocalyptic John James Audubon. "Last night, again, the US military base was loud with the sound of helicopters and airplanes taking off and landing," he writes.

"As the anger of people across East Asia grows into an anti-American struggle, it'll be harder for the US military to do whatever it wants." I'm not so sure.

H. and his comrades believe that war games are not a deterrent but, rather, pure provocation. "Things feel more dangerous than usual," he tells me. We talk about South Korea's growing weapons market and—over lunch at a buffet patronized by soldiers, construction workers, and taxi drivers—watch news of Pyongyang's latest missile tests on a wall-sized TV. We talk about the pitiless, hot war in Ukraine and what feels like something much warmer than a cold war between China and the United States.

It's November, yet I'm wearing a T-shirt and SPF-50 sunscreen because the temperature is around seventy degrees Fahrenheit. Too hot for Korean cabbage to grow, endangering the local kimchi supply, but just right for me to have taken a morning swim a few days earlier—breaststroke and freestyle and aimless floating—in the ocean far, far south of here. I do not tell the activists why I keep traveling down to Busan. I feel guilty about my time on the beach, my US citizenship, the exchange rate that's tilted so heavily in my favor, the family members and friends who have served in the US Army and are thus able to sign me onto the bases that the activists believe to be stolen land. In less than two weeks, I'll stuff my suitcases full of dried seaweed and anchovies and sundry notes on militarism, and board a commercial flight back home, straight into the gut of empire.

Ill at ease in the motherland,

E. TAMMY KIM

UNITED STATES ARMY GARRISON HUMPHREYS, PYEONGTAEK, GYEONGGI PROVINCE, SOUTH KOREA

DEAR McSWEENEY'S,

In Las Vegas, grasshoppers have begun to show their faces, the crackling of their exoskeletons echoing through the city's empty spaces. Deep within one of the Strip's best hotels, a Hollywood production crew worms through a hidden maze of hallways and loading docks, ferrying cases of equipment to set up a world-class production.

Contestants will begin arriving at any moment. No one dares to name the show quite yet. Production assistants and crew members alike dash around with frantic looks.

The city's airport has recently been renamed after a lifelong Nevadan democratic senator, but otherwise nothing much has changed. The baggage claim carousels remain nestled between slot machines and a singular dilapidated chain coffee shop. Giant screens pay homage to the city's offerings. The colorful ads reflect on the satin floors, all a wet shade of gray.

Contestants and their parents and guardians emerge into this fantasy throughout the day. Eyes wide, cheeks flushed. Apart from musical instruments and pieces of luggage, all contestants have an air of naïveté. To be here is to be plucked from obscurity, to be one step closer to fame and surprise. The show allows only young adults to pass through its doors. Regardless, only a certain kind of kid can afford to bite.

Next to the baggage claim, a woman listens in as a group of contestants chats away. The kids anxiously recount the day's journey—the plane tickets emailed the day before, the clothes they forgot to pack, the song they've put all their money on. The woman captures every detail.

"You guys can't take pictures, can you?" the woman asks one of the contestants.

"No, not today. Sorry!" responds one of their guardians.

"No worries. I guess I *will* tune in this season."

None of us dares to whisper the name of the show, the delusion. To say it is to believe it, after all. Contestants go down two sets of escalators and into a small passenger van, in which they will travel along the city's back roads. Who won the contest last year? Nobody knows. Yet the contestants' eyes glimmer with excitement, captivated by the lights of the Strip. Reality has not fully set in.

Months ago, I responded to an ad for an assistant position at a top production company. The description was simple: a week-long job on reality television. Having spent months alone drowning in my own thoughts, I was looking for ways to escape. Last week, an unknown number appeared on my phone. The memory of my application was long gone. The voice on the other end of the call told me all I needed to know. Perhaps I, too, am here for the way the show's name rolls off the tongue.

My job is to handle the celebrity judges. To bring their coffees, seventeen-dollar smoothies, three glasses of celery juice, and skinny margaritas to set. It is my job to look away when their eyes fix on my face, should they ever do that at all.

Mornings are the most magical. At the crack of dawn, the crew lines up their personal vehicles by the valet and moves in unison toward the ground-floor elevators. We must rise to the third floor, fetch our radio systems, shuffle past the restaurant, make a left, and take another set of elevators to our assignment: up to the thirty-second floor and make a right at the bar to do interviews; up to the sixth floor and make a left at the spa to escort contestants to film the poolside B-roll. Today my target is on the fourth floor, at the end of the hallway.

She is the first judge of the day, dressed to perfection in bright green pants and a purple crocheted flower fashioned as a top. Her makeup is matte on her face, set to withstand hours under studio lights. Her entourage exchanges morning chitchat with a producer as they move down the hallway like one unit. I'm invisible, in the back, informing producers of the judge's every move in an unencrypted text chain.

At the elevators, I am supposed to usher everyone into an empty car, then hold back until a new one arrives. I do as I'm told. When I return to base camp, on the third floor, I run past the restaurant and catch up to the judge's entourage.

She holds her phone above her head. "I *am* wearing a flower! Don't you love flowers?" On the other end of a FaceTime call are her toddler and her husband. Yearslong celebrity lore populates in my brain. *It can't be him, there's no way*, I text a friend.

Over the shoulders of her makeup artist, head of security, and stylist, I catch a glimpse of his face. His features, pixelated, barely fill her screen. I've only ever seen him in movies, on posters adorning friends' childhood bedrooms. His face matches the voice I know, the accent scrambling out of the phone mere feet away. I tell myself I've just FaceTimed him. I text friends, I send cryptic tweets.

Later, when it's time to transfer the celebrity judge's smoothie into a non-branded coffee cup, I say her name. It's the first time we've spoken.

"Would it be better if I put the smoothie in a clear cup, then add a sleeve to your coffee? That way you don't have to think about which one is which."

"Yes. Thank you."

She's so sweet, I text the group chat. Perhaps the delusion has taken over me too.

At the end of the day, when the elevator doors open, playback filters in from the judges' room. "It's a yes from me," one judge says. "It's a no from me," goes another. Their lines echo in the empty studio. No contestant is there to hear them.

Until next season,

LILLE ALLEN
LAS VEGAS, NV

DEAR McSWEENEY'S,
I write this from Buenos Aires, my dearly missed hometown. On this day, December 15, Argentina has just qualified for the World Cup final. For those who know the meaning of soccer (fútbol) outside the United States, it goes without saying that people here feel as though they are experiencing a truly magical and historical event—the streets sizzle with energy and speculative hope, passants absentmindedly whisper hooligan chants to themselves, and you can't walk for more than a minute without seeing someone sporting a Messi jersey. On Saturday I spent a lazy afternoon watching England v. France from my house, whose balcony overlooks a street near a crowded intersection. I didn't hear a single conversation that wasn't about soccer. People were dreaming about the national team. The country was obsessed.

In *McSweeney's* 68, I read Alejandro Zambra's fantastic essay—or story, depending on whether you believe his or his wife's words—on soccer sadness. In it, he explains the particular memory of being a kid in Latin America and seeing your father cry after a loss. For Zambra (and most of us), these were perhaps some of the few instances when rough men showed themselves to be emotional and sensitive; they were cathartic moments for a contingent of people who were trained, above all, in quietness and sober patience, in disciplined stoicism.

I know a bit about soccer sadness myself. I was born in 1996, a year before the titan of soccer Diego Maradona retired. Maradona's promising heir, we were told as children, was this kid called Lionel Messi, who, at age thirteen, had both a terrifying hormonal disorder and an unseen amount of talent. Messi was very short, agile, and matchless in his dribble, and was sought after by European and Argentine teams alike. In 2001, the year of the worst financial crisis in Argentina, no team in his home country was willing to pay for Messi's hormonal treatment. So while the core of the country's capital was exploding—with bloody protests in the streets that left thirty-nine dead and had the president fleeing the Casa Rosada

in a helicopter—Messi left for Barcelona.

It's not easy to describe what followed. For years, Messi created wonder after wonder for Barcelona FC, winning tournaments and Ballons d'Or, achieving the arguable status of "greatest of all time." In the meantime, his game for Argentina's team kept floundering. Playing irregularly at best, he was left out of the starting lineup in the 2006 World Cup quarterfinals, when Argentina lost in penalties against Germany. Although in 2009 Maradona, as a coach, bestowed on Messi the honor of wearing his own number 10 jersey, Messi couldn't click with his team, falling once again in the quarterfinals against Germany, this time with the embarrassing final score of 0–4. His closest shot came in 2014, during the World Cup finals, but here Messi and his compatriots fell to Germany yet again, and he returned home to Barcelona, hanging his head. During this time, he also lost three Copa América finals and was uninspired in the round of sixteen during the 2018 World Cup.

There is a famous tango that says: "First you learn how to suffer, then to love, and then you part ways." Although the tango speaks about some early twentieth-century lover, the words ring true when we think about Messi on the Argentine national team. For years, the promised "Messiah," as people called him, seemed frustrated, unable to mesh with the players of a country that saw him as an outsider. Argentine journalists responded with their signature cruelty, claiming publicly that he should play for Spain; some of his countrymen despised him; Messi even left the national team for a spell. Having lived in New York since 2017, I felt disappointed, albeit mirrored, by the struggles of this young man who didn't know how to return home.

First you learn how to suffer. I flew back home last week, taking off shortly after the Netherlands scored two goals against Argentina and went to penalties. The plane was dark and everyone was silent. Then magic ensued: the pilot announced a victory over the Netherlands, and passengers burst into chants, beating their jerseys in the air, recalling the name of Messi, rightly, beside that of Maradona. The relief was immediate, and justified by years of patient, disillusioned waiting. There is nothing like that unapologetic, collective joy—nothing, regardless of where you're watching or where you are from, will make you feel more a part of something

than sharing the unabashed passion of Argentine fans.

Yesterday, after beating Croatia, innumerable crowds in the city met up to celebrate in a state of delighted communion. Children who could barely speak waved and sang on their parents' shoulders, and teenagers climbed the streetlights to steal kisses from one another. In Bangladesh, an unexpectedly passionate crowd celebrated until the wee hours of the morning, and Argentines reciprocated by waving the Bengali flag. My American fiancé's mother, hardly a soccer fan, told us she had inexplicably shed a tear. I saw my fiancé himself suddenly metamorphosing into an Argentine, singing along with an accent and childlike exhilaration.

Kafka writes in his aphorisms that the messiah will come only when he is no longer necessary. We learned how to suffer, we lived without Messi, and now he's arrived. I am writing this after the pure elation of chanting in the streets for many hours straight, and I don't know whether we'll win the World Cup or not. You, my reader, have an unspoken advantage over me: you know whether this letter ends in ecstasy or eulogy. But above all I would like to leave a testament to what Messi's last World Cup has been:

a true state of fútbol; a way of coming back home; and, above all, a form of soccer joy, of soccer happiness.

Besos,

JULIA KORNBERG
BUENOS AIRES, ARGENTINA

DEAR McSWEENEY'S,
Actor Dar Dixon was, to put it politely, pessimistic about my peace project idea. More precisely, he said it was "never going to happen" and referred to me several times as "fucking crazy." He was one of three people who responded to the hundreds of letters I sent seeking donations, so maybe he was right. As the husband of Donzaleigh Abernathy, the daughter of Reverend Ralph Abernathy (who, with Dr. Martin Luther King, led the civil rights movement), Dar was curious: "Where did this activism come from?" I don't remember exactly what I said—probably something about my passion for social justice. Dar said, "No, that's not it!" Again and again, he asked, and rejected all my answers. He didn't think they came from the heart. Finally, I told him, "I don't like bullies." He said I was getting closer, but it was apparent I hadn't examined my life particularly well. I pondered his question for weeks.

Slowly I unearthed clues about how I became who I am.

I remembered my mother urging me to watch violence on TV, trying to toughen me up. Bloody bodies of soldiers in Vietnam splayed on the ground were nightly news fare, and Walter Cronkite ended every newscast with "That's the way it is." But did it have to be? I remembered my cousin Ronnie, home on leave from the war, chain-smoking, trauma in his eyes.

I remembered a Friday-night slumber party. Thirteen-year-old me and my classmates camped in the living room of Shirley Pollow's home in Fitchburg, Wisconsin. We ate popcorn, drank pop, and pretended we were competing in the Miss America pageant. We wrapped sleeping bags around our bodies in a semblance of evening gowns. We giggled and sashayed around the room as if we were on a runway. Eventually we tired and collapsed in front of the black-and-white television. Our laughter stopped. The evening news was broadcasting live from Chicago, in what later became known as the Days of Rage. Protesters running. Police chasing and clubbing people. Cars ablaze. It was October 10, 1969.

We sat wide-eyed. Chicago was over the border, only two hours away. Were we safe? University students in Madison, just five miles north, regularly protested. My nineteen-year-old cousin, Sheila, was one of them. Was she protesting at that very moment? We watched as protesters risked jail, injury, and possible death. The protesters believed ending the Vietnam War was more important than their safety. I was fearful but in awe. They were my heroes. I was envious of Sheila, who was old enough to do something, to actively engage in protesting.

Growing up near Madison, Wisconsin, during the '60s, I couldn't possibly have remained untouched by the anti-war movement. Two years before the Days of Rage, Dow Chemical had arrived on the University of Wisconsin campus in Madison to recruit students for jobs. Dow manufactured napalm and Agent Orange. What started as a peaceful protest turned into a riot. Friends of my parents stopped referring to university students simply as "students." They became "rioting students." Protesters regularly smashed windows. In response, businesses boarded them up. This was along State Street, from the student union to the capitol, block after block. Layers of anti-war flyers papered telephone poles and any other surface students could get their hands on.

Now the unrest was palpable. Madison felt like it would erupt again at any moment. (Less than a year later, it did, when the campus's Army Math Research Center, which was involved in aiding military efforts, was bombed.)

In 2019, on the sixty-fourth anniversary of Emmett Till's murder, I found myself driving to Emmett's gravesite. I had told my best friend, Frannie, that I thought I was supposed to be there that day and invited her to come along. Always ready to accompany me as I follow my "nudges from the universe," she immediately said she was in. When we arrived at the Burr Oak Cemetery in Alsip, Illinois, we were overwhelmed by the enormity of it. Frannie noticed a Black man watching us as he approached on a golf cart. I ran over and asked him for the location of Emmett's grave. He wouldn't make eye contact. He wouldn't respond. I waited. We must have looked like two suburban white women who had no business being there—especially not on this day. I understood his reticence. Not long before, the Emmett Till memorial in Sumner, Mississippi, had been riddled with bullets. Obviously, the man was intent on protecting Emmett's grave from

harm. I waited. After a few minutes I said, "I brought flowers."
Finally, he turned to look at me
and searched my face. Then he
said, "Follow me."

We waited on the roadside.
A small cluster of people at
Emmett's gravesite eyed us with
suspicion. It took several minutes
before they invited us to join them.
All of them, it turned out, had
family ties to Emmett. They were
about to begin a libation cere-
mony. Generously, they asked us to
take part. I felt I was meant to be
there, but why? Maybe it was to
show Emmett's relatives that they
weren't alone, that grief reaches
across racial lines. Maybe it was
for me to take even more seriously
those "nudges from the universe."

When I talked about my visit to
Emmett's grave, surprisingly few
people recognized his name. I felt
I needed to do something to pre-
vent his story from becoming lost.
Then I learned about peace poles.
The first was installed in Japan
in 1955, the year Emmett was
lynched. It was created by Masahisa
Goi, who had been influenced by
the atomic bombings of Hiroshima
and Nagasaki during World War
II. Now there are more than two
hundred thousand peace poles in
180 countries. They all proclaim
the message MAY PEACE PREVAIL
ON EARTH, usually in several

languages. I learned there are more
than sixty languages spoken in Ela
Township, in Lake Zurich, Illinois,
where my home is located. I also
learned that our state's first Ku
Klux Klan rally was held here in
1921. A cross was burned, and
more than two thousand members
were initiated. I thought, What
better way for our community to
acknowledge its sordid history
and express its desire for reconciliation than by dedicating a peace
pole to Emmett Till, marking
the hundredth anniversary of the
KKK rally? Then, on the last day
of Hanukkah in December 2019,
two local schools were defaced
with swastikas and words of hate.
Residents were outraged. The time
seemed ripe for a peace pole.

Dar asked me, "Don't you
know where you live?!" Somehow,
he had intuited the pervasive
racism and xenophobia in my
community, while I had lived here
for forty years and was oblivious
to it. No sooner had a group of
us, Democrats and Republicans,
formed the Ela Peace Project
than we were called left-wing
propagandists. Celebrating our
community's diversity and including every language spoken here
on a peace pole—this was decried
as partisan. The spokesperson for
the local Lions Club repeatedly
tried to kill our project. When

we talked about the 1921 KKK rally, people became angry and asked us to stop speaking the truth about our town's history. We were thought to be intent on damaging its reputation. One village administrator accused me of wanting to celebrate the KKK! We refused to be censored. Then we were told we should put the project on hold. We were told, "People are upset about George Floyd. You should wait until they calm down." The "people" referred to weren't upset that George Floyd had been *murdered*. They were upset because there had been protests, and people were openly talking about police brutality/murder and racism. It hadn't occurred to me that our community might not embrace a peace pole. Obviously, I didn't know where I lived.

Just as Dar had predicted, raising money proved extremely difficult. Shopkeepers felt that affiliation with the peace project would cause them to lose business. One synagogue was interested in donating, but wouldn't until a church donated first. Not a single house of faith ended up donating, nor any of the local foundations, nor any of the five municipalities within the township. Then the pandemic hit, making it even harder to raise funds.

Donzaleigh Abernathy urged, "Don't give up. Don't you *ever* give up." And we haven't. And, fortunately, the Ela Township Board has stuck with us through every controversy and complaint, never rescinding its support. And now, after more than three years, the peace pole has been fully funded and is in the process of being fabricated. At fourteen feet tall, with the word for "peace" in all the sixty languages spoken here cut into its stainless-steel surface, it will stand as a beacon for peace on Main Street in Lake Zurich. But it will not be dedicated to Emmett Till, nor will it be tied to reconciliation for the 1921 KKK event. One hundred and one years later, our community is still not ready to make peace with its past. If the peace pole is not immediately vandalized, I will be surprised. But if it is, that, too, will become part of our community's story.

I remember how my idealism infuriated my father, who thought it would lead only to disappointment. He wanted a realist for a daughter. But I remain idealistic. I continue to hope and strive for a better world, as I follow "nudges from the universe."

Peace,

SHARI GULLO
LAKE ZURICH, IL

PURPLE MOUNTAINS

by PATRICK COTTRELL

OUTSIDE MY APARTMENT WINDOW, a blinking neon sign. This morning I watched a crew of men install it and one of them caught me staring. Three puffy clouds sat on the tips of a dark purple mountain range, jagged and pointy like a cartoon. My neighbor, the one who liked to make small talk in the mailroom, said he thought it was for a strip club or a bar.

Last summer I ran into him in the hallway and he invited me over for a private piano recital. Around 7:00 p.m., I heard a knock at my door. I crouched behind my sofa and didn't answer. After a few minutes, I could hear him playing scales on his piano, signaling that it was time for me to come out of my apartment and join him. Instead I slipped away, an hour later, to run an errand. On my return home, as I stood outside my building, I looked up and saw him sitting in his window, talking to no one, and he seemed lost. Like a lost man.

When the men were done installing the neon sign, after they had packed up their tools and taken down their ladders, leaving bottles with urine on the sidewalk, I walked to a bar to have some drinks. I should have invited my piano neighbor to make up for the fact that I'd bailed on him and his private piano recital, but I didn't want to tell him about how I'd been doing nothing with my life because I was on a break from teaching, just sleeping and reading. No writing or anything productive. It took me an hour to reach the bar, a mile away. Inside, there was one woman sitting on a stool.

"I suppose you don't like sports," she said to me.

There was a basketball game on the flat-screen TV up on the wall. The players ran into one another and flopped over in what seemed like a repetitive, plaintive, punishing male ritual. I said she was right: I didn't like sports or pay attention to them; perhaps I should've so I'd have something to talk about. She said she liked how people have to react physically with their bodies. One's ego can't take over when you have a split second to respond to an external stimulus.

The bartender came out from behind a swinging door. I ordered a whiskey. It tasted like the smell of the fabric seats in my grandfather's Buick. The woman who liked sports introduced herself. Her name was Susan and she said she was a writer. I didn't tell her I was a writer too. I kept it to myself. I asked Susan what she wrote about, but she didn't want to talk about it. She wanted to know if my childhood was pleasant. I began to talk about the Midwest, the prairies and grasses and my adoptive family's history, but she looked bored. "Where is your favorite forest?" she said. "No," I said. "I don't have one." She asked me if I wanted to step outside the bar with her and smoke cigarettes or weed.

"Tomorrow I'm getting a divorce," she said.

One of the main reasons I declined to step outside the bar with her to smoke was that I had already smoked a lot of weed that day. The bartender asked me if I wanted another whiskey and I said yes.

"My husband moved out and into one of those long-term-living hotels. He took a lot of my things," Susan said.

"I always thought my parents should've divorced," I said.

"Have you tried meditation?" she asked. "What was your true face before you were born?"

"Meditation makes me more anxious," I admitted.

"Not everything is for everyone," she said. "Personally, I like to keep my house clean."

I was listening to her and watching the basketball game. One of the players—the tallest one, with shoulders that stuck out like an alien's—fell down. His knee was bent back at a ninety-degree angle and everyone was crowded around him, waiting to see if he could stand up. If my knee bent back in a public space, no one would notice or care. I had never played team sports. I had never joined groups. A former therapist of mine suggested I join a support group for Korean adoptees. I avoided group work and lacked a team mentality and a sense of community or connection, whether with Korean adoptees or queer or trans people. I didn't belong with the Christian, Korean adoptee population, and I even took time to repeat my story to the therapist, who had already heard it, about how I had been on a panel of Korean adoptee writers, and how out of place I was, how I'd felt like the audience and panel members appraised me as an oddity, as not fitting in with the general vibe of upper-middle-class, liberal-leaning churchgoers who liked book club books. I remembered that when the panel was over, there was a table for signing and no one came up to me except one Asian woman in casual business wear who said she thought I seemed angry about being there. She suggested I smile more often.

"Are you meeting someone here?" said Susan.

"Rikki," I said. I made up a name. I thought it sounded good.

"Do you think Rikki would want to go to a reading later?"

"I'll ask her. She might bail on me. She can be a flake."

The reading was at a bookstore a few blocks from the bar. Five or six people had come, which amazed me because I had never heard of this author, and, in general, I tried to keep up with contemporary writing. Instead of standing at the podium, the author, an Asian man, sat in a circle with us. He held the book far from his face with one hand and gestured with the other. It turned out the five or six people in the audience all worked at the bookstore. I bought his book. I wanted to support another Asian writer. It was his second novel; I heard him tell Susan it was not as good as his first.

Now that Susan and I had begun the evening together, it was difficult to say when we would go our separate ways. It was always difficult like that with a new person. I thought we'd have to offer to give the author of the evening a tour of the city's drinking establishments, and when he said he was exhausted and depressed and wanted to go back to the hotel, I was grateful. Susan kept walking with me. She didn't ask me where we were going. I walked into my apartment building. I could hear my neighbor playing the piano. The last time I'd seen him, he'd told me he was writing his own compositions; his creative work had to unfold organically or he'd rather not play at all. He said he felt free now. He seemed disappointed that I didn't ask follow-up questions. Susan followed me upstairs and into my apartment.

When I closed the door, Susan, as if she had been worried the author would overhear us, asked what I thought of his reading. I said it was good, but I hated imagining the author having sex with a woman, which is what we'd had to do when we listened to him read that night, because that's all he wrote about. I was one of those people who always imagine the author as the narrator when they read. I couldn't help it.

"So what's your friend Rikki doing?" Susan said. She sat down on the couch.

"I'm sure she's fine."

"How do you know her?"

"Grad school. We stayed in touch. She's just a person I know. It's not a big deal."

Susan smiled as if I were joking. She asked me if I had a girlfriend.

"Not at this moment," I said.

"What's wrong with you?" she said. "You seem normal, besides the fact that you've probably been depressed your entire life."

"I'm not depressed," I said.

She asked me if I ever went up into the mountains. She said it was the main benefit of living in this city, being so close to the mountains. I told her it scared me, the idea of driving up there and getting trapped in the snow. She said it wouldn't matter. I had heard the weather changed quickly and you needed chains for your tires. Besides, I didn't own a car. She thought it would be good for me to drive up into the mountains, to take in the views. The vastness might be clarifying, but she didn't explain how. In the summer sometimes she went to Greece or Barcelona. Had I traveled? I was more of a hermit; I had not traveled.

"But do you *want* to travel?"

"Not necessarily," I said.

"You should learn how to ask for the things you want. And if you don't want to ask, just say them out loud. Speak them into being."

She said it was like that with writing: your characters need to want things. It can be more than one thing. In fact, the more things they want, the better. More desires mean more complications. I could see how she would be a good teacher. She was attractive and charismatic, and she believed in what she was saying.

"I'm not a writer," I lied, and then I asked her if she was hungry. She said no. She looked around my apartment, but there wasn't much to see.

"Can I borrow that?" she said. "My husband took mine."

She pointed out the vacuum in the corner of the room, an old upright model from the '80s. I had stolen it from my parents' house in Wisconsin. I didn't think they'd miss it. They never noticed much, but sometimes they asked me if I was depressed because I was adopted. Sometimes they asked me if I was upset that my brother died. They noticed things like that.

"Sure," I said. I didn't care too much about the vacuum.

"I should get going. My daughter will be getting home soon."

Susan sounded very sad.

"I have a lot to do too," I said.

Susan ordered an Uber. She gave me her number. I carried the vacuum down the steps and stood outside and waited with her. She smoked a cigarette even though she admitted smoking made her somewhat of an outcast in Denver, where everyone was so focused on wellness.

"I don't really know you, but I'd like your opinion," I said to Susan.

Because I was lending her my vacuum, I felt I had the right to ask her for something. We were standing underneath the neon sign. We looked up at the neon purple mountains. During the day the sign looked shabby and run-down, but at night it was luminous and bright.

"I'm asking you what you think this sign means."

"What do you think?" she said patiently. She sounded like a teacher.

I said that all day I had thought it meant nothing, then tonight, very suddenly, I'd realized it was a reference to a singer-songwriter named David Berman, who recorded his last album under the name Purple Mountains. It must be referring to him and his work. He took his own life in Brooklyn, on the night before his tour was supposed to start. His friend, a famous writer, found him. I hoped she had never heard of David Berman, so I could tell her more about his life and work. I didn't know anyone who liked him or even knew about him. My ex-girlfriend thought his voice was annoying. But some people loved him.

"I don't think so," said Susan. "It's a mountain range. It's where we live. Anyone can see that."

On Friday night I texted Susan to ask her when she wanted to meet up. The next morning I woke up to the sound of my neighbor playing one of his new piano compositions. I checked my phone and imagined a text from Susan appearing. *Yes*, she would write. *I would like to meet very soon. As soon as possible.* Waiting for someone to respond is like a bad trip, I thought. When my brother was in his mid-twenties, he took his own life. I've come to think of it as my sad story, the way my brother died, the simple fact of it. Whenever I thought about his death, I felt heavy. If you're on a bad trip, my cousin told me once, you have to ride it out. If you keep telling yourself you're on a bad trip, it will make things worse.

At the end of the summer, I decided not to return to teaching. It was confusing to be at the center of a classroom. There was too much ego involved. I never understood why people listened to me. After a couple months of searching on Craigslist, I found a temp job in an office, and on weeknights I cleaned the bathrooms at a Catholic high school a few blocks from my apartment. When I got home, I smoked up and sat on my couch. Susan's ass sat on this couch, I thought one night. It was dumb, and I was embarrassed I wrote it down. Susan never wrote back. When I looked at our text conversation, I saw my message asking her to meet up and nothing else. I was on a bad trip and I knew it.

A year later, I was living with my girlfriend. We had met online. She was a computer programmer and spoke almost no English. We lived in a condo in Huntington Beach. One day we went swimming in the ocean. I didn't have anything to do that day, or any day, except live with my girlfriend. She was supporting me financially, but she didn't seem to mind. I overheard her tell our neighbor in the hallway that I was an easy man to live with. Anyway, I think that's what she said. It was a good arrangement. I had everything I needed.

That day at the beach, the water was cold and dramatic. The air was sharp. Brightness upon brightness searing my eyelids. My mind flashed to Susan and how she'd said that taking in the view of the mountains could be clarifying. I tried to remember what she looked like. We had spent half a day together, if that. I'd always been bad with faces. I tried to picture the girl who'd sat next to me in sixth-grade English class. Her name was Erin Mars. She'd racked up numerous absences. I'd let her copy my homework. I couldn't remember the face of the woman I had spent half a day with, or the face of the chronically ill girl with whom I had spent a year. What I remembered most clearly about all the instances was my own generosity and kindness.

After an hour in the ocean, my girlfriend and I relaxed on the beach. I looked around and couldn't see anyone who looked more relaxed than the two of us, spread out on our beach towels. My girlfriend sat up and handed me a container of organic strawberries. I was eating them when out of the corner of my eye I saw a large black blob flowing toward us, larger than a whale.

It took me a minute to realize that the blob was a team of synchronized swimmers. I watched at least fifteen or twenty little old ladies in black swimsuits go through an entire routine as if they had been rehearsing it all their lives. Maybe they had been. Everything was leading up to this instant, this moment of the swimmers performing their routine in the ocean. I was staring at them, admiring their strong and precise movements, how each movement led naturally into the next one, with nothing extra attached. No ego or desire. How decisive they were as a unit. How they'd come into the ocean with a plan, and the precision with which they were executing it. I didn't see a coach or a conductor or a team of assistants. I couldn't stop watching. My girlfriend noticed. She pointed at me and said one word: "Creepy." I think that's what she said.

"I want to live a long and uneventful life," I said to her. "Just so you know, that's what I want."

"Right," she said, nodding. "Okay."

She smiled, laughed. She was laughing. There was this day, the next day. My understanding was that she felt sorry for me.

AN EGGNOG

by TOVE DITLEVSEN

Translated from the Danish by MAYA SOLOVEJ

THE CHILD STOOD BY the back stairs with both hands gripping the banister, bent over it, entirely still, listening for the front door opening and closing below, and distant steps she imagined were her mother's, right until they stopped a few floors down and the slam of a door once again shattered her hope.

Now Hansen, on the third floor, had come home; and Ketty from the soap factory; and the stoker Henriksen's wife, who worked at Carlsberg with Mother and, naturally, would come up to tell her if anything had happened. But maybe she couldn't bring herself to, or she simply didn't know. Almost every day an ambulance wailed off with someone—it was, after all, such a huge factory.

Ill at ease, she stepped hard on her own toes and stayed like that for a long time, so that her tears, dripping heavily all the way down to the basement, would have a tangible cause. It was like this every day, for a shorter or longer while, depending on how late her mother was. She always went to the same spot to listen, a bit before anyone could reasonably expect her mother to arrive.

Her white face shone blank and inert, like a dimmed flashlight in the dark. Behind the open kitchen door, one could hear the low burble of boiling potatoes. In the modest living room, the table was set for two. The flowering geranium had been moved to the oilcloth's center; this always brought out her mother's pale, familiar smile, because a flowerpot belonged on the windowsill, not on the dinner table.

Just as the child released her tight grip on the banister and sat down at the top of the stairs, defeated and crying loudly, as if to show fate that she had endured enough and deserved a break, she heard the gate open, and a slight, imperceptible sound, maybe just the scrape of a shoe against the courtyard's cobblestones, made her leap up and, in a feverish, inexpressible fit of joy, rush into the kitchen, switch on the light, and turn off the potatoes: Mother was here! Now she was returning her bike to the shed, now she was climbing up the stairs, closer and closer. The child's world filled with light, her heart with peace.

She had her back to the door, with her hair like two black wings down her cheeks, and was putting the steaming potatoes onto a plate, when her mother came in, slamming the door behind her.

—Whew, so cold out there.

—I fried the meatballs, Mommy. They just need to be warmed up.

Her voice was raw, like a pubescent boy's. She wasn't much smaller than her mother, but as scrawny as a sick dog because she was left all day to fend for herself. Her face was small and perpetually worried, with a pointy chin and a grayish, unhealthy complexion. Only her eyes shone large and dark blue and serious in her little grim face.

Her mother did not respond, and neither spoke until they were seated at the table, and her mother, with a pale, sweet smile on her made-up face, put the enormous geranium back on the windowsill. When she sat down, she accidentally bumped into the naked bulb, which swung back and forth, casting shadows on the faded wallpaper.

She ate quickly, two deep furrows between her narrow, plucked eyebrows. Her bleached hair was a dark, indefinable color at the roots and had no shine, just like her tired, near-sighted eyes. The days had been so alike over the past decade, she had scarcely noticed the transformation that had happened to her face. Red blush on her cheeks and lips, a dirty powder puff dabbed on, and a little black brush swept across those thin eyelashes; before the mirror, in the gray morning light, time seemed to stand still, and each day was like the last. If she ran out of blush, she bought more, and there was enough powder to cover her ravaged face with white for an eternity, and enough thirsty men in the world for the stream of empty bottles to pass pitilessly down the assembly line faster than her quick hands could catch and rinse them clean. You could call her life sad, but when she complained, it wasn't so much because she recognized life's sadness, as something done simply out of habit, and because it was seen as proper to fuss over everything. In its way her life really was secure, because of all this powder and all these thirsty men, and sometimes it was good, because of the child, whom she seldom spoke to.

While she ate, the child observed her. Her mother left in the morning before she woke, and these precious hours before bed were the only time they could be together.

The child had no memory of her father. A sailor is always a guest in his own home, and besides, she was only three when she last saw him. She harbored the same inevitable hatred toward him as her mother. Maybe that, too, was just the result of convention and habit. —That bastard, said the wives at Carlsberg and on the stairwell. —He better not show his face here again, added her mother. But the child's hatred was mute and arose from the protective tenderness she felt for her mother.

Once they had eaten, she cleared the table and rinsed off the plates. She would wash them the next day when she came back from school.

Her mother's purse lay open on the kitchen counter, a few coins scattered about. The child regarded money with a mixture of awe and resentment. To earn money, her mother was gone all day. Money was the cause of unending hours of labor, anxiety, and loneliness. Each penny cost a bit of Mother's strength and some of her strained eyesight, ruined from constantly holding bottles up to the light to make sure they were clean.

She hadn't been very old when she asked her mother why she went to work when it was so much nicer to stay home. Then she was told it was to buy food and clothing for them, and that Sunday the child had nervously asked if they would go without food since her mother was home.

She wondered why the purse had been flung so carelessly on the counter and hurried to pick it up. She was dropping the coins back in, when she suddenly sensed her mother behind her. She gave a start because she hadn't heard her coming. Confused, she let go of the purse and with her forearm she swept the hair from her face and met her mother's strange, mistrustful gaze. She became bright red and stared at her mother with huge, frightened eyes, which made her mother's expression fill with rage, then defiance and uncertainty, until a shadow of shame crept over her face, and, no longer able to bear the child's terrified expression, she turned away, half-ashamed and half-annoyed, and went back into the living room.

The child stood frozen, silent, beside the purse and the dirty plates. Her breath quickened, her thoughts tumbled one after another behind her hot, pale forehead: She thought I was trying to steal, she thought I was taking money from her—maybe she thinks I've done it before—as if I didn't cost her enough already—if only that purse hadn't been lying there—if only everything could be the way it was— dear God, let everything be the way it was—let it not have happened.

What are you standing out there gawking for? her mother yelled from the living room. Her voice was irritable and strange, as her eyes had been, with a hard, aggrieved quality that guarded against the regret and tenderness she had never learned to express. She pulled out a sewing kit from the sideboard behind the table and at last covered the glaring bulb with a rag. Then she sat before the stained tablecloth and pulled out a worn sock and stared at it as if wondering how a single sock could have so many holes. Anxiously, she listened for sounds from the kitchen, her rough red mouth twisted into an expression of torment. She did not acknowledge that anything unusual had happened, but an uneasiness grew in her heart, like when an animal senses danger and lifts its head in attention.

Then she called the child by name in a gentle, strange voice that sounded foreign even to her. The child came in and sat across from her with an uncertain glimmer of hope on her little thin face, like the one she'd had when she stood in the dark on the back stairs and imagined that the steps she heard were her mother's, until a door slammed somewhere else in the building.

She's going to say something now, she thought.

The silence in the room pained her. She glanced nervously at the heavily ticking clock, as if the sound could stop the redemptive, unknown words hovering on her mother's lips. Vaguely, the child felt that these odd, unspoken words had to come from her mother, not because she was wrong, but because the child could not manage alone. She couldn't say,

I didn't steal. Partly that would make it real, and one could never again imagine that nothing had happened, and partly those were the words of a thief—no one could keep her from using the same words if she really had stolen, or thought of it. This new and unexpressed truth made something knot up inside her, and conjured terrible glimpses of the injustice she might one day be subjected to.

Mouth agape, she fixated on her mother's lips. Those too-red and rough lips that rarely quivered with emotion, whose contours were never softened by tender and loving words. A factory girl's hastily kissed and discarded mouth.

She is still staring at the sock, as if she has forgotten what to do with it. She experiences the child's silence as pain, shattering the good existing order. She doesn't quite know what has happened, but the child's distress reaches her through secret and unknown pathways. Thoughts cross hopelessly in her mind. She doesn't know that we can always help the one we love. She meets the child's gaze. And her eyes are pleading and scared, as if she, too, were a clumsy child who had smashed a precious vase on the floor. Then she clears her throat and says gently, —Why don't you make yourself an eggnog. And she sees the pale, pointy face relax and break into a smile. The child jumps up with a flutter of her long, straight legs, and rushes to the kitchen.

—You should have one, too, Mommy. I'll whip one up for both of us.

Calmy, she takes up the sock.

SERRANOS

by FRANCISCO GONZÁLEZ

THE TRAILER PARK WAS our domain.

We were nine sets of parents, with a dozen children. On the other side, we had all lived in the same village. Now we lived in Ranch View Mobile Estates, on the outskirts of Buellton. The owner had posted a sign at the entrance that said FIXER-UPPERS AVAILABLE! and another that said THIS COULD BE HOME! We knew because our children, who were literate, had told us.

At Ranch View Mobile Estates, there was no code enforcement and no regulation enforcement. A scattering of oaks and sycamores fought for their lives among heaps of used, broken, empty things: huge propane tanks, PVC pipes, busted stoves, crippled tractors. When we walked around our neighborhood, we did so with the occasional sound of shattered glass crunching underfoot.

But the trailer park was a good place to raise children. Each family had its own Shasta, Forester, Kenskill, or Spartan. Rent was only a few hundred dollars per month. And the entrance could not be seen from the county road, which made it difficult to find, even if you'd been told where to go.

A wall of corrugated tin surrounded our five-acre community. We had fashioned secret exits along its perimeter, where we'd loosened the bolts that joined the sheets of metal. In the event of a raid, we could jiggle the bolts, slide a panel, and take flight into the woods.

Although we had been ten years in the valley, and no longer thought of ourselves as foreigners, our precautions had long ago become a part of us. We avoided banks, police stations, doctors' offices. We had stopped attending Mass, since we'd heard the stories of worshippers seized at the steps of churches. And we visited Albertsons or Safeway only in groups of three at most. We couldn't risk losing too many adults; someone had to remain to watch over our daughters and sons.

We were civilized people. We were not like the migrants who stumbled through the valley, alone or in small bands. They'd wander the roadsides, begging for work in alleys or parking lots. They'd toil a week or two on ranches. Now and then, we caught sight of them sleeping rough in the shade of trees, in creek beds, or beneath bridges. Very few of them managed to harden to the labor, put down roots, and endure as we had.

* * *

When the strangers walked into Ranch View Mobile Estates, we thought they'd arrived by mistake. There were eight of them. They lugged fifty-pound packs, bedrolls, and polyester blankets; they wore huaraches on their feet. We nearly approached them to ask if they needed directions, but they knew where they were going. They had keys to the vacant Holiday Rambler and began to move in.

The Holiday Rambler was one of those enormous 1960s trailers. It had a makeshift plywood porch. Its broken windows were boarded up, and its flanks blackened by a fire that must have burned before our time. We were shocked that human beings would make that rig their home.

At first glance, the strangers all appeared to be young men in their early twenties. But then we noticed a woman among them who had long gray hair. Her presence eased our fears. If the youths had traveled with an elder and taken care of her, surely they couldn't be so bad.

Nevertheless, we agreed that the worst thing you can have in your proximity is other people. We observed the strangers' every move as they made improvements to the derelict trailer. They pulled the weeds that obscured it. They chased away the family of possums that lived in its undercarriage. They unboarded its windows and used old rags to shine its corroded aluminum exterior until the trailer looked bigger, and parts of it reflected light.

* * *

The strangers knocked on our doors and made their introductions. Rather, it was the gray-haired woman who introduced them, while the seven young men stood behind her in silence. The woman wore a woven cotton dress with the sleeves torn, and a crimson rebozo around her shoulders. She moved and carried herself like a prizefighter in the ring. She seemed to be in charge.

She said, "I am Mother Paz. And these are my sons."

Immediately we were skeptical. The young men did not resemble their supposed parent, nor did they resemble one another. That, and Mother Paz appeared far too old to be their mother. Despite this, when she referred to them as "sons," she sounded so confident that none of us could bring ourselves to challenge her.

One by one, we presented ourselves to our new neighbors and shook their hands, which were every bit as rugged as ours. It was hard to communicate with the young men. Their words were plated with an accent we didn't recognize. But Mother Paz spoke for them, and she spoke our language well. She told us they had come from the Sierra Madre de Chiapas.

"So you're Serranos," we said. "Tell us, how bad are things in Chiapas?"

This was a rhetorical question. We knew about the peasants who had risen up against the government and been crushed. We knew about Subcomandante Marcos, and Red Mask, and the massacre of Acteal. It was the stuff of legend.

The old woman, who styled herself a mother, grinned at us, and yet we detected a gloom passing behind her eyes. We could tell she was pretending not to be upset, so we pivoted.

We asked the Serranos if they needed jobs. We explained that we earned our keep three miles up the road, at a boutique winery of some renown, where grapevines crowned the terraced hills. The winery also had horses, hens, and goats. We cared for the animals, and we cared for the grapes; we poured samples for tourists: reds, rosés, whites.

We mentioned that our boss might need a few extra hands, since it was now April, and fruit would soon appear on the vines. "We can set you up," we offered, "as long as you deliver." We didn't know what sorts of people grew up in the southern mountains, or what manner of work they'd be skilled at, but we hoped we might win them over by doing them a favor.

Mother Paz shook her head.

"Thank you, but we have all of us farmed for the last time."

Arrangements had been made: they would work at the new Greek restaurant.

The Greek restaurant was on the far side of Los Olivos, which meant that the Serranos had to commute more than six miles each way on foot. They left in the small hours before dawn and got back after dark. We predicted, correctly, that their routine was not sustainable.

A few weeks into it, we were all dining at the picnic tables at the center of the trailer park, when the Serranos approached us. Mother Paz asked if we knew of an easier way to reach Los Olivos—a bus, perhaps. No, we assured her; there was no public transportation in this corner of the valley. We were used to walking to the winery, and our children were used to walking a half mile to their high school.

Mother Paz snapped her fingers. "I should have known— there's always one stitch in the rug that I miss. I've got another idea, though."

She'd heard about the Department of Motor Vehicles. She and her sons would probably go there and obtain driver's licenses. If they saved for a few months, she figured they could buy a used car. Nothing fancy—something small would do.

We couldn't stop ourselves from laughing. We informed the Serranos that they wouldn't be driving on California roads, not in this lifetime. Only citizens were allowed to have licenses. And even citizens had to take tests, fill out forms, and speak English if they wanted to get behind the wheel of a car. The process was so convoluted, so overfilled with restrictions, that it would be simpler to hijack a crop duster and fly to work instead.

Mother Paz was incredulous. "Those rules are absurdities!" she cried.

Again, we laughed.

"You're not wrong," we said. "Even so, you're in the North now, and every dance is a different dance."

* * *

The following Saturday, the Serranos left the park in the chill of dawn. When they returned several hours later, they were walking single-speed bicycles with knobby tires. The bicycles were teal or hot pink or lime green, and low to the ground. Some of them had tasseled handlebars; clearly they were built for kids.

We didn't know how to ride bicycles, and neither did our children. It was immediately obvious that the Serranos didn't either, though they wasted no time in trying.

They practiced in the evenings. Three or four of them would roll through the trailer park, pushing themselves along with their feet, while the rest used flashlights to illuminate the path ahead. We were glad they had sense enough to wear helmets. Some of the riders managed to lift their legs for a few seconds, but they seemed to spend most of their time crashing to the ground and shouting words that we assumed to be profanities.

Mother Paz, who was clumsier than the rest, crashed so many times that her helmet finally broke in two. The young men helped her up, and she shook dirt from her dress.

"Remember the proverb," she said: "'The Devil fell and lost his grace, but not his pride.'"

Minutes later, she was at it again.

In the days that followed, the Serranos began to add accessories to their useless bikes: reflectors, baskets, luggage racks, bells. A few of them tied artificial roses to their top tubes. Then came the American flags, the miniature ones you could buy at Walmart; the Serranos attached these to the backs of their seats.

There was something particularly annoying about the flags, which seemed to imply that we needed to be reminded of where we lived. Or perhaps the Serranos were foolish enough to believe that stars and stripes would save them if they got in trouble in the world beyond Ranch View Mobile Estates.

Spring gave way to an early summer. Squashes and tomatoes ripened in the fields on either side of the county road, and grapes swelled in the vineyards. It wasn't hard then to ignore the Serranos. Our shifts were longer and busier; visitors flocked to the winery in buses and expensive cars. Our boss would lecture them on acidity, tannins, and flavor compounds. Meanwhile, we'd hustle back and forth with fresh glasses and bottles, getting them drunk. Some of the tourists seemed to shit money. The older they were, the more they drank, the more they tipped us.

On Friday afternoons, we'd line up at the front office, and our boss would pay us in cash. He'd remark that Spanish people were good workers, and we were confused as to why he would say that, because we had never met anyone from Spain. When we asked our children to explain, they rolled their eyes and said, "He's too stupid to live."

Our children transacted mysteries that were beyond our knowledge and past our learning. They were good at English, so good that they could memorize rap lyrics. They could even identify peculiar accents just by overhearing a few words; they'd gesture at chattering tourists and tell us, "That man is probably from France," or "That one sounds British."

On Sundays, our children read the local papers to us, translating on the spot. They'd decode the content from cover to cover. Gossip. Sports. Crime. Politics. It made us giddy to see these displays of intelligence.

Sometimes our children would ask us, "Do you ever wish you could read? Or speak perfect English?"

And we would joke, "We wish you couldn't. So you'd understand what it's like for us."

One day, we returned from the winery to find the Serranos riding their tiny bicycles through the trailer park—without crashing. The seven young men rode single file, with Mother Paz leading them, and they were all whooping and laughing. Somehow they'd solved the puzzle of balance.

We stood there watching the Serranos. They formed an odd parade, with their American flags fluttering behind them. One of the young men had duct-taped a portable radio to his seat post and was blasting country music. Mother Paz glided past us, cackling. She looked almost like a witch on a broomstick.

The spectacle of the bicycles so excited our children that some of them began to clap and cheer for the Serranos, but we found this irritating and demanded their silence.

* * *

Every weekday morning, we trudged to work on the shoulder of the county road, while our neighbors followed the same road to Los Olivos on their bicycles. They usually passed by without saying much, which was fine with us. We had no real desire to converse with them. We would have preferred to keep them on nodding terms, at most.

Occasionally, though, one or more of them would slow down to match our pace and spoil our mood with talk. They boasted that it now took them only thirty minutes to reach the Greek restaurant, "or twenty, if you really step on it." They could visit any of the surrounding towns: Santa Ynez, Ballard, Los Alamos. They'd been to the Santa Maria Target, where the aisles were so long that you couldn't see the end of them. And they'd been to a theater in Solvang, where they'd watched a movie about a million penguins mating. The movie had inspired them. Someday, they said, they might try their luck at crossing the mountain pass into coastal Santa Barbara. They had never seen the ocean, but wanted to.

Privately, we agreed that the Serranos were idiots to put themselves at risk in their petty adventuring. We were content to keep a low profile and focus on our work. While we moved drip tape, mucked corrals, and sprayed chemicals between the vines, we'd fall back on our fantasies. Our children would grow up to be suited professionals, stacking money. With a little luck, we would end up living in their two- or three-story houses. Then there would be nothing left to do but play with our grandkids, push their strollers, and rest our bones.

In June, the Serranos invited gabachas into the trailer park. The gabachas were roughly the same age as the young men, and drove not bikes but ramshackle cars. They'd pull into our community and stroll past us as if they had every right, as if we were furnishings in their living room. Sometimes they brought plastic bags of mota and six-packs of beer, and they'd sit on the porch of the Holiday Rambler, drinking and smoking with the Serranos. There were at least four or five gabachas, though they were hard to count, because we couldn't tell them apart. They all had brown hair with blond highlights. They all wore lipstick and short skirts, and had tattoos. They'd all get drunk and talk too loud, and when they laughed, they'd tip their heads back and open their mouths wide, like donkeys.

The Holiday Rambler had next to nothing in the way of insulation, so we could tell right away when the sex began. On weekends, pairs of Serranos and gabachas would enter the trailer in shifts, and we could hear their coaxing, moaning, and grunting. The Holiday Rambler's walls jounced and swayed until we wished it would collapse. But it was built to last.

We decided to make our displeasure known to the Serranos. Since we were conscious of our numerical superiority, we agreed it would be best if only three of us approached them. A group of that size could impart seriousness, without the implicit hostility of a larger crowd.

On a Saturday morning, the chosen three of us found Mother Paz sunbathing on a lawn chair beside the Holiday Rambler. She wore a pair of sunglasses, a high-waisted bikini bottom, and a T-shirt with Superman leaping out of it.

It was a small matter, we said. But did she think her boys could be a touch more discreet? With their exchanges?

We had decided beforehand that *exchanges* was the most suitable word in our arsenal. Its vagueness would spare the conversers from directly acknowledging the dope, the boozing, and the carnality.

But Mother Paz only said, "You know how young people are."

We had hoped for a simple conversation. Briefly, we considered whether this woman's grasp of our language was really as strong as we'd thought. Then we noticed the telltale rocking of the Holiday Rambler starting up, and, along with it, the braying of a gabacha. This prompted us to say that yes, youths can forget themselves, and they can forget their neighbors, and sometimes it takes an elder to set them right again.

Mother Paz removed her glasses and folded them.

"Scripture tells us that love does no wrong to a neighbor, and therefore love is the fulfilling of the law."

We were struggling to keep our cool; we were in no mood for a religious debate.

"Our children look up to you," we admitted. "You're showing them things they shouldn't see and shouldn't hear."

"I'll take that message back to my sons. But I can't make any promises."

When we instructed our children to keep their distance from the Serranos, they asked us to explain why.

"They seem to be hardworking people," we said, "but we don't want you to be entangled in the things they do when they're not working."

"They're really nice to us, though," our children said. "We play Lotería or soccer with them when you're not around. And Mother Paz brings us baklava from the restaurant."

"She's nobody's mother."

"Who cares? She's our friend."

"Why not make some real friends, kids your own age? When school starts again, invite some classmates over—we'd be happy to meet them."

"Our classmates avoid us. They say we smell like trash because we sleep in a landfill."

"This is a trailer park, a neighborhood. They should know the difference."

"Difference? What 'difference'?"

Our children became furious. They were sick of spending empty summer days surrounded by rubbish, explaining obvious facts to us. They suggested that we were jealous of the Serranos since "you're boring, and they're fearless. And you can't control them the way you control us."

We were hurt, and sad that our influence was no longer

what it had once been, but we were not entirely surprised. Our children had entered their teens, and we had expected defiance on their part. Some of our coworkers at the winery, the ones who lived in other communities, had shared stories of their sons and daughters dropping out of school, experimenting with narcotics, dating hoodlums. We couldn't imagine that our children would sink so low, but they were bound to find new ways of testing us. Naturally, we were tempted to punish them. Our own parents wouldn't have tolerated such flagrant disrespect. They would have taken belts to us, or whips, or electrical cords—whatever happened to be within reach. In the end, though, we kept our hands down and let our children be. This was a phase that would pass in its own time.

Grape tending kept us occupied well into the evenings. We trimmed clusters, discarding immature fruit. We planted bell beans, oats, and daikon beside the vines to lure away insects. The air was heavy with the scent of fresh manure and turned earth, which smelled to us like prosperity and renewed our optimism.

One night a commotion woke us from our shallow sleep. There was the sound of something like whistling and popping, and we noticed intermittent bursts of light coming through our curtains.

"Stay inside," we told our children. "We'll handle this."

When we opened our doors and stepped out, we were horrified: the eight Serranos—along with a few gabachas—were shooting bombettes and flash powder and multicolored jumping jacks. They were spinning flame wheels and fiery balls that screamed into the air. An immense plume of smoke had risen from our neighborhood.

"Stop!" we begged. "Stop all of this!"

Mother Paz came forward.

"Friends, it's *Independence Day*," she said.

We tried reasoning with her. Hadn't she heard of *zero tolerance*? The fireworks were illegal. And they were especially dangerous at this time of year, when a single spark could set the entire valley ablaze. The display was visible for miles around. If a malicious outsider should see it and call the police, we'd all be taken away.

We implored Mother Paz to trust us and benefit from our advice. In order to persist in the North, you had to hush your impulses. You had to withdraw from the world until nobody gave a damn about you.

Mother Paz delved into our faces; there was no shame in hers.

"I've been told that tonight is a night to celebrate. Maybe you should relax for once."

Enraged, we told her, "Maybe you should live in a place where you don't have neighbors, so you don't have to act like neighbors!"

"All right, fuckers! I don't know anything about anything—is that what you want to hear?"

The seven younger Serranos had been observing our exchange. From their wide-eyed expressions, we could tell they understood our anger, if not our vocabulary. Mother Paz turned to them, barked something in their language. They extinguished their firecrackers, and the gabachas followed suit, until all was dark again.

That weekend, the Serranos avoided us. They stayed behind the door of the Holiday Rambler.

On Sunday evening, we held a meeting in the Becerra family's trailer. All eighteen of us crammed ourselves into the kitchen/bedroom/living room.

We said, "These Serranos have come to spread chaos! They're pissing on us, and we're kneeling here with open mouths!"

Only one set of parents dissented, counseling forgiveness. "They're our brethren," they said, "not our adversaries. Haven't we all crossed the same border? Aren't we all just workers following the work?" They suggested that this was a teachable moment for our children. This was an opportunity to put a good lesson into their hearts, and into the hearts of our neighbors.

The rest of us wouldn't have it. Our animosity was only hardened by that sort of talk. Forgiveness be damned— those beasts hadn't even apologized. And it wasn't our job to teach them how to apologize, or think, or be passable humans. Now was the time to stand up, raise our voices, and yield no ground.

We said, "If it comes to battle, so be it: we have the numbers!"

We would tell the Serranos to pack their bags. We would order them to leave Ranch View Mobile Estates immediately.

All eighteen of us marched across the trailer park. Since we wanted to appear as formidable as possible, we had changed into our best pants, guayaberas, and dresses—the things we'd worn to one another's weddings, our children's baptisms, and weekly Masses, back when we were still brave enough to attend church. A few of us also strapped machetes to our hips. They were tucked into leather sheaths, and we didn't plan on using them, but we thought they'd add considerable authority to our demands.

We intended to give our neighbors the type of shock they wouldn't forget. Candlelight flickered in the windows of their trailer, the focal point of our wrath. When we reached its porch, we assumed the most vicious expressions in our power, and pounded on the door. It swung open.

A gust of warmth and humidity escaped the Holiday Rambler. We were greeted by Mother Paz and her sons. They wore aprons and chef's coats. Behind them, on a small table, sat a host of saucers and bowls caked in flour. Pepper stems and seeds were piled neatly on a rectangular cutting board. We saw wooden spoons, spatulas, and dough scrapers soaking in a washbasin.

Three of the young men held a massive earthenware pot.

They lifted its lid, and gesticulated in a way that said, *Have a look.*

The pot contained several dozen rectangular dark green pouches, which were fat and smooth and beaded with moisture. They looked like vegetables from another world.

Mother Paz noticed our bewilderment.

"Some tamales for you, prepared in the southern style," she said. "They're wrapped in the fronds of a banana tree. Don't wait too long—eat them while they're hot."

A few of us tried to speak, but we couldn't bring our denunciations into being. We were stupefied.

Food is sacred to our people, and has been for numberless generations. Its presence governs our behavior. You can't attack someone when they've cooked fresh provisions for you and opened their hands; tradition tells us that it would be as bad as striking down the healer who binds your wounds. Maybe the Serranos were aware of this, or maybe they weren't. In any case, we were constrained by our principles and unwilling to commit sacrilege.

So when at last we found our voices again, we had no choice but to thank our neighbors. We accepted the earthenware pot. Of course we hadn't forgiven Mother Paz and her sons, and our differences were far from settled, but they had pulled our fangs and bought themselves time. We divided the strange tamales between us—half a dozen per family— and returned to our homes, dressed in our finery.

* * *

The tamales, which had been made by this so-called mother and her so-called sons, were the best we had ever eaten. Their flavor bloomed in stages. Beneath the leaves, the cornmeal was soft and buttery. This was followed by a tangy second layer that surprised us with a hint of tamarind. The most intense delight lay at the core of each tamal, where a spicy flourish whispered across our taste buds.

Our children ate with us. They asked, "How come you've never made tamales like these?" and laughed when we had no answer. We considered that perhaps our ancestors had passed down the wrong recipes, and these were the first true tamales we had tasted; maybe all the rest had been mockeries. We licked and scraped the banana leaves, extracting every trace of their essence. It was happiness pumping through our bodies.

Our neighbors were uncivilized. They were unpolished. But you don't need so much polish when you're sincere.

The Migra came for the Serranos on the ninth of July.

They had raided Santa Ynez, southeast of us. And they had been seen in Buellton. Still, we hadn't expected their agents to bother with a town as small as Los Olivos, which had only a thousand inhabitants. For some reason the Migra—or else the town itself—wanted to make an example out of the Greek restaurant.

The details oozed into our knowledge from various sources. We learned them from coworkers at the winery, and from cashiers at Albertsons, the ones who spoke our language. And our children told us what they could, when the *Santa Barbara Independent* printed a brief article about the raid.

We listened as our children translated: The raid had happened around 6:00 p.m., during the dinner rush. The Migra had taken ten restaurant employees into custody. They had fired two shots in the process, since a few suspects had resisted capture. One suspect had been hospitalized with "minor injuries."

Our children turned a page, then another, and frowned.

"There's nothing more—that's all it says."

An amateur photographer had been dining at the restaurant at the time of the raid, and we examined the black-and-white photos she'd snapped. You could see trucks and vans and pistol-wielding agents with bulletproof vests, who were escorting three handcuffed men out of the restaurant. The young men must have been taken completely by surprise; they hadn't even removed their hairnets or their latex kitchen gloves. They'd averted their faces from the eye of the camera, and we couldn't make out their expressions, but we recognized them as our neighbors.

Our children announced their plan to walk into Los Olivos.

"We're going to check things out," they said.

They pointed out the fact that only three Serranos had appeared in the paper. Maybe the other five had eluded the Migra and gone into hiding. Maybe they needed help.

It took us a few moments to realize that our children were serious.

"This is a game to you?"

"We should go," they said. "We're American-born, and we can't be taken away."

"Don't be so sure!"

We recited the names of friends and relatives who had thought they were safe but had vanished all the same. We stressed that men, women, and children were known to die in Migra prisons. And captives died just as often when sadistic agents turned them loose in hellholes like Agua Prieta, Reynosa, and Ciudad Juárez, where people like ourselves were food for wolves.

"At this rate, the newspaper will run an article about a gang of thumb-suckers who should have listened to their parents!" we said.

Our children held their ground. They crossed their arms.

"This is the right thing to do, and it's the least we can do for our neighbors," they said.

We couldn't back them down, so we began to beg. We wept and wailed. We embraced them and refused to release them.

Then, too, we were proud of our daughters and sons, even though we wouldn't reveal it. The years had sculpted their character. They were so strong that siding against them was like siding against nature. Someday perhaps we ourselves would be dragged away, and they would need that strength to survive in this country without us.

Our children's voices softened.

"If the Migra got their hands on you, we'd scour the earth," they said. "We'd find you, no matter what."

And with that, we let them go.

Raided businesses often make a show of reinventing themselves. After several expeditions to Los Olivos, our children reported this to be the case with the Greek restaurant. For a week, it stayed dark inside. Then a crew of workers undertook a series of renovations. There was a lot of drilling and hammering, lifting and moving. The workers repainted the facade, and it became powder blue instead of brown. They replaced the plastic OPEN sign with a neon OPEN sign, which was bright enough to be seen from down the block. They filled holes in the parking lot, paved it with fresh tar, and etched new lines between the parking spaces.

In the second or third week after the raid, the gabachas reappeared at Ranch View Mobile Estates. Sometimes they sat alone on the porch of the Holiday Rambler, hugging themselves. Sometimes they came in pairs and loitered together. When they spoke, they spoke in murmurs. Every now and then, they'd try the door, even though they already knew it was locked. Perhaps they just wanted to touch something that their lovers' hands had touched.

A month after the raid, our children informed us that the Greek restaurant had started doing business again. Its double doors were propped open. A large banner appeared across its awning. It said GRAND REOPENING in big letters, and UNDER NEW MANAGEMENT in smaller ones.

The Holiday Rambler's curtains remained closed behind its windows. There were days when clouds rumbled, and their sprinkling brought up nettles and smutgrass around the trailer, until it appeared to be sinking into the weeds. We could still see the path leading to the home of our erstwhile neighbors, which had been imprinted by the weight of their comings and goings. Abandoned laundry fluttered on their clothesline, and when night becalmed the breath of the trailer park, we could hear T-shirts slapping against pant legs.

Our children stopped looking for the Serranos. But they couldn't stop dreaming about them.

In one dream the Serranos lived in a zoo, where each of them was housed in a small cage with steel bars; when you got too close, they'd roar in the way that mountain lions roar.

In another dream Mother Paz couldn't see you, even when you stood right in front of her. She'd wander around the trailer park muttering, "Almost."

Our children tossed and turned in their sleep. They woke up gasping, and we kneeled beside their beds, held their hands, and soothed them just as we had when they were babies. We told them they need not worry. The Serranos were nothing if not resourceful; they were quick on their feet. "And wherever they've ended up, they're surely together," we lied.

When our children were out of earshot, we confided our true feelings to one another. The dreams had provoked in us a new sense of disquiet. They were exactly the sorts of dreams you might have about the dead, when they reach out from the hereafter.

Now when we went to work, we slogged through the woods and up the Santa Ynez riverbed, which is parched all but two months of the year. August was the height of rattlesnake season, and we had to watch our steps, but none of us wanted to follow the county road anymore. We felt endangered by the eyes of passing motorists.

A harvest day arrived, and we rose before dawn to prepare ourselves for long hours among the vines. While our children were fast asleep, we covered up with hats, bandannas, neckerchiefs, and long-sleeved shirts. We packed coolers with food and water and gathered at the picnic tables. We were about to leave.

Just then, we spotted Mother Paz.

We were terrified at first. If someone had told us that we were seeing a wayward spirit, we would have believed them. But Mother Paz was really there, riding through the entrance to Ranch View Mobile Estates on her pink bicycle with its American flag. She rode alone. She wore no helmet, and her long gray hair swirled freely in the wind. We were astonished—somehow she'd escaped.

The Migra worked in mysterious ways. Once, in Lompoc, they'd barged in on a wedding banquet and took more than forty people, but spared the singer and his band. Another time, they'd raided a plum orchard outside Los Alamos and arrested only the male workers, leaving the women behind. It was hard to discern any logic in their doings. Agents took parents and left children; they took children and left parents. Perhaps they had decided that Mother Paz was old and would die soon anyway, and did not think she was worth their trouble.

The violet sky advised us that we were supposed to be at the vineyard, yet none of us made a move. Mother Paz dismounted her bicycle a stone's throw from the Holiday Rambler and let it fall to the ground. Her face was dirty. She looked barely awake and far away; she was panting like the wounded.

Stupidly, we asked, "Where are your sons?"

Mother Paz brushed past us without a word. She must have hoped that the events of the last several weeks hadn't been real and that the young Serranos would be waiting for her, and she didn't have any space in her thoughts for us. She pulled a key from her pocket. A moment later, she hobbled into her home.

We acted strong, enclosed in the trailer park, but we knew we were prey. Neighbors brought our fears to life. It was easy to hate them; we couldn't bear to love them, since they never lasted long. The heat of day was upon us, defining our shadows as we approached the Holiday Rambler. We decided it would be enough, for us, not to be forgotten. Gently, we knocked on the door.

THIRTY-SIX VERY SHORT STORIES

by SPARROW

THE CURIOUS CASE OF DR. FINNEY

A HOUSE CALL

MY DOCTOR CAME TO visit me. I hadn't called for him; he just came. (Dr. Finney is a holistic practitioner.)

I invited him in, and he whipped out a deck of cards, then fanned them out, upside down.

"Pick a card, any card," commanded Dr. Finney.

I picked a card at random.

"What card is it?" he asked eagerly.

I showed him the three of clubs.

"Your health is excellent!" the doctor decreed. Then he retrieved the card and left.

THE RETURN OF DR. FINNEY

Three months later Dr. Finney returned to my house. (Again, I had not called for him.)

"I've been in prison," the doctor confided.

"What f-for?" I stammered.

"I was framed for embezzlement," he answered, with a conspiratorial smile.

"How was prison?"

"Expansive," he remarked. "When you contract your physical space, your soul expands."

Then Dr. Finney turned and left.

LO MEIN

A few days later Dr. Finney reappeared at my door holding a Chinese takeout container. "Would you like some lo mein?" he asked. "I bought too much."

"Sure," I replied. I got out a bowl and he poured some noodles into it. Then we sat at my table and ate.

The food had a strange taste, like chopped-up branches of a tree.

"This lo mein tastes unusual," I remarked.

"Yes, the chef is also a master herbalist," Dr. Finney replied. "This food will cure your tendency toward constipation."

He was right. I was never constipated again.

THE TOWEL

Four days later Dr. Finney returned with a red towel. "Use this towel the next time you take a bath," he explained. "Not a shower, a bath."

"Can I pay you for it?" I asked.

Dr. Finney screwed up his face. "Yes, pay me what you think it's worth."

I gave him thirty-five dollars. Dr. Finney looked uncertain.

"Can you make it thirty-eight dollars?" he asked finally. "I like numbers that end in eight."

THE TOWEL, PART TWO

I used the towel the next time I bathed. When I passed it over my head, my hair turned blond.

For two days I was blond.

THE EXPLANATION

The next time I saw Dr. Finney, I told him: "Your towel turned my hair blond."

He nodded. "I'm not surprised. Probably you have always had an unconscious desire to be blond. That towel responds to unspoken wishes."

SHOPDROPPING

Shopdropping is when you enter a store, surreptitiously pull out an item from your pocket, place it on a shelf, then hurriedly walk out.

Shopdropping can be more disruptive to a business than shoplifting.

CONFESSIONS OF A TINY METHODIST

I live in the town of Cotownchel, in Switzerland. Life is quiet here. We have one bookstore, which sells only books about scuba diving. Half the town is addicted to scuba diving (in the Greek isles); the rest of the town is deeply religious.

I am part of the religious community. I am a Tiny Methodist. I go to a tiny Methodist Church, which has room for only three or four people. If five people cram into the church, there is trouble. Sometimes it takes two hours for us to extricate ourselves; it's like a game of Twister. But usually only two or three people attend: the minister, the organist, and one congregant. The organ is extremely loud because it's right next to one's ear. From outside, our sanctuary resembles a doghouse. Yet, ironically, no dogs are allowed.

FLYSWATTER

Two men were walking down the street. "These damn flies!" said one.

"Don't swat them," advised the other. "That just makes them bolder."

"I don't care. I'm swatting them," insisted the first. And he brought his hand down with a resounding slap onto his own left thigh.

"I quit drinking coffee and they stopped bothering me," asserted the second, whose name was Yancey.

Kleb, the first man, was silent—a silence composed of contempt.

"Are you hungry?" he said finally. "Want to eat some oysters?"

"No. Oysters are slimy," Yancey murmured. He stopped and stared into the eyes of a cat. The cat appeared to be psychically connected to another planet.

For a long minute, Yancey and the cat communed. Then Kleb slapped at another fly, and the cat ran off.

"You're just slapping yourself; you're not hitting them," Yancey remarked. "The flies are laughing at you."

"I cannot hear their tiny laughs," observed Kleb.

GOD'S TELEGRAM

"God is constantly telegraphing His love for you—but you don't know Morse code!" snickers Swami Vasilananda.

THE TORTOISE AND THE HARE

The tortoise and the hare played a game of basketball. Slowly the tortoise dribbled to his end of the court, lifted the ball, aimed, and threw. The ball went through the hoop!

Meanwhile, the hare had scored 312 points.

MOVIE CONSTELLATION

If each movie actor is a "star," six of them together are a "constellation."

HISTORICAL OVERVIEW

"Darwin freed us from the tyranny of religion," Bartholomew observed. "Now who will free us from the absolutism of science?"

INTENTIONAL SHIT-STEPPING

"I have never stepped in dog shit intentionally," Rhonda said. "I'm not sure I could!"

MY LITERARY CAREER

My failure as a poet hasn't stopped me from also being an unsuccessful novelist.

NEW CAT

"I bought a second cat so my first cat would have someone to hate," Angie strategized.

GHOST MEETINGS

When I die, I'd like to be buried in a huge cemetery where you can meet lots of other ghosts.

COUS

I made half a pot of couscous—in other words, cous.

HIGH TIME

"When I see someone I know, instead of saying *Hi*, I say 'High,'" Vincent disclosed. "No one ever notices."

MARITAL STATUS

My wife is both married and divorced.

THE STRUGGLES
OF THE RICH

"My furniture is so lovely, I feel grotesque," Annalee gasped.

THE BLESSINGS
OF THE POOR

"My furniture is so ugly, I feel gorgeous," Morris giggled.

PENTANGLE ENDORSEMENT

"A love triangle can be treacherous, but a love pentangle is remarkably stable," Amy assured me.

CONFESSIONS OF AN ADULTERER

"I don't particularly like sex, but I love disguises," Matthew* dictated.

*Not his real name.

BARGAIN HUNTER

"I seek out bargains—not to buy them, just to admire them!" Henley bubbled.

SUCCESSFUL CRIMINAL PETITION

Criminals petitioned the United States Postal Service to stop putting their pictures up on post office walls, and on August 3, 2006, the USPS agreed.

SEEKING LISTEN SHOWS

I'm tired of talk shows. I'm looking for a listen show.

THE DECLINE OF HUGGING

I used to hug people three times: when we met, when we

parted, and in the exact middle of our conversation. Since the age of COVID, I never touch anyone—not even myself.

ONE SECRET

I dress like my enemies.

PARADOX

I am kind to strangers, but strangers are still rather hostile to me.

PHILOSOPHER-FASHIONISTA

Only philosophers understand fashion.

LAWNMOWEE

"The term *lawnmower* suggests that there's also a *lawnmowee*," Paul discoursed.

DANCING
CLOTHING

"Choreography is a way of making clothes dance," Agnes de Mille synthesized.

ONE-SIXTY-FOURTH

We have the phrase *half smile* in our language, but not *quarter smile*—let alone the rare but intriguing *one-sixty-fourth smile*.

SUSPENSE

"I'm reading a suspense-murder-thriller-horror novel called *After the Daisies Die*," Edna reviewed.

POSTCARDS TO THE DEAD

It seems possible to send postcards to the dead. Letters, of course, cannot reach the next world, but postcards, with their colorful images of autumn leaves and Egyptian monuments, probably can penetrate the veil of death.

Tomorrow I will send a card with a picture of Coney Island to my deceased uncle Joe.

WOUND BOUND

by SARAH WANG

WEDNESDAY. TODAY I THREW Micki's toothbrush into the trash. An LAPD diver descended into the Tar Pits to retrieve a murder weapon used in an unsolved homicide. There were huge gas bubbles rising to the surface of the tar, which the diver popped with both hands. I read that in the paper, stolen from the office after breakfast. We're not supposed to read the news in here. But Lola and I decided it's important to stay on top of current events and not let ourselves get too disconnected. Couple nights ago, I had a dream about being in the woods and finding the journal of a missing girl with the words *Wound Bound* written in it. What does it mean? Today Lola's boyfriend came to visit and smuggled in a green notebook for me, shoved into his baggy jeans. If we want to write, we have to do it on loose sheets of unlined paper and turn it in for assessment. Being here is like running on the edge of a dream. All day long I imagined popping that tar bubble with my own two hands, grabbing a column of it and squeezing, kind of stretchy and solid-feeling, the air inside existing as its own thing—not just as air, but as a distinct entity with its own purpose.

Thursday. They found the toothbrush in the trash. Dragged me out of group. You have no proof, I said. This is not a court of law; the clinical supervisor scribbled a report. So now I have to go to bed at seven. Who goes to bed at seven? The seniors' ward, maybe. I'm just lying here writing all this in my new green notebook in the leftover light from the parking lot. If I stand on the bed and jump really high, I can see the lot out the window. Yellow lights. A Honda Civic. Daewoo. Day woo. *Woo*: to try to gain the love of someone (typically a woman).

I'll tell you about Lola. She eats only one stalk of celery a day. Well, she used to. Now they make her eat, and if she chews up a slice of bread and drinks from her carton of chocolate milk, they don't write down in the daily report that she's insubordinate. Then she throws it up in the shower. What can they do? It's her body. She's sixteen, two years older than me. The girls in her group home finger each other on the dryer when they're doing laundry in the basement. Hot and rumbling on their asses. Lola says it's the best. I bet. I can feel it, too, so hot it burns. Shooting up my spine, making me glow, a red shelter. When she and another girl from the group home ran away, they lived in a tunnel by the riverbed for a week, shoplifting, eating sliced meat from plastic packages with their fingers. Then they caught Lola and brought her here. The other girl went to juvie. Lola showed me how to throw her gang sign, plying my fingers into crossed Vs in the mirror, pressing her chin into my shoulder as she stood behind me. She kissed the scratches on my arms and oiled them with pats of butter pocketed from the cafeteria. I'll die if she gets out before me. On the outs, we're going to steal a car and drive to Baja, where her cousins live. Baja. I think of whales and carbonated beaches; blue, blue gemstone water. Lola behind the wheel of an old truck, long dirt roads kicking dust, desert on one side, ocean on the other. What I like about Lola is that we're the same person, not the way we look or what we do but everything else, everything that matters.

Paneled ceiling of pocked particleboard. Lying in bed morning after morning, waking up here again. During group, staring off at what qualifies as our sky. In the nurses' station, the cafeteria, the common room, where we watch old DVDs, the same sky prevails. I see patterns in the random data: crumpled horses, toothless mouths. Skinny tubes of green fluorescence. A cherubic plastic spoon, our only utensil.

Saturday. Yesterday was so bad. So bad. After my mother left, I stayed in bed. No dinner. I said I was sick. If they'd made me get up, I would've eaten a chunk of my own shit and gotten myself sick. For real. Then what. That's what the kid did, the one who they kept throwing in the padded room. Family groups are the worst. Joley's mom and dad just sat there breathing. They don't speak English, so they couldn't participate, but the courts require them to attend. Darnell doesn't have family, only his fosters, but they don't come for anything. Lola's mom has a missing tooth and long, beautiful hair. I wonder how she gets it so shiny and straight. She fell asleep while she was talking. It's not sleep, Lola said. She's a junkie. She nods. Lola is the opposite of her mom. She weighs seventy-five pounds and her face is just skin stretched over a skull. The wildest thing that happened in group was when Cordy got so mad, she stood up and crossed the big circle of chairs to the other side, where her mom and sister were sitting, and kicked her mom in the knees. She looked like a nice lady, but I don't know. They're all assholes pretty much when you find out the real story. Straight up, they shot Cordy with five milligrams of Ativan and strapped her down in the padded room. After group, we all went out there and took turns standing on chairs and put our faces in the little window to kiss the glass. For Cordy.

My mother said in front of everyone that I was the devil's spawn, like some religious freak. She's not even religious. I can't take it anymore! she said. Ungrateful! No respect! She climbs out the window at night. She's pomegranate! They all looked at me like, *WTF?!* I knew what she meant—promiscuous—but I kept it shut. Boys, you know! I wish she didn't speak any English at all, like Joley's parents. Marijuana! Lazy! Sleep all day! Kick her out! Tough love! Then the parents all clapped, even Joley's. How can people not see how hysterical she is? I mean, they see it, but they think it behooves her, because how else should a mother behave when her daughter is a pomegranate and locked up in a loony bin? What they don't know is that she's the one who makes me so nuts I can't stand being alive, which is what brought me here in the first place.

The only time I got out of bed yesterday was for Dr. Garbian. He is a mop, super skinny with gray yarn hair. How do you feel today? What I really had on my mind was running through the ward pushing people over, and once they were down, crushing their bodies with my giant feet, walking all over them, feet as big as twin mattresses, one foot for each of their bodies. What did I say out of my mouth? I'm angry. What makes you angry? Dr. Garbian doesn't look at me as he scratches his yellow pencil on his yellow pad. My mother. What about her? Everything. He says I should write it down, but I won't do that. Because the truth will not get me out of here. Because I will never tarnish this journal with lies. That's for other places. Lies to get out of bed. Lies to make you forget. Lies to make you a mother. How about this, then? He looks at me with soapy eyes and I look away. Write down what makes you angry. No. He sighs. Write down what makes you sad. Okay. That's easy.

· When I was a kid, I had a little toilet that I sat on for hours. There was a silver key my mother wound on the side of the toilet and music would play. She set up a long mirror in front of me, propped against the wall. I sat there making shapes with my fingers, the music tumbling around and around as I watched myself, the reflection in the mirror the opposite of shadow.

- Doug selling ecstasy out of his bedroom window at his grandma's house after his parents kicked him out.

- Sitting in the treehouse after the kids I was babysitting went to bed. Me and Magda rolling greasy condoms we stole from the parents' bedroom onto bananas and throwing them into the ravine.

- Pressing my face on the cold white metal frame of my old bunk bed.

- Cruises. Fireplaces. Spanish houses. Taiwan. My father. My sister. Her husband. No teeth. All mothers. Ceramics. Karaoke. My birthday. Chinese soap operas. Asthma. Steroids. Child support. Night school. Kahlúa and milk.

- Adohr Farms milk, the only crap they give us to drink in here. In 1916, some guy named Merritt Adamson established the dairy farm in Tarzana, California, naming it after his wife, Rhoda. *Adohr* is *Rhoda* spelled backward.

· When Elma's cousin drove her and Magda and me up Angeles Crest Highway to a trail where a severed head had been found the week before by a hiker's dog; the rest of the body was never recovered. We sat on a cliff and watched the marine layer cover the basin, a dream hugging the earth.

Lunch. Gotta go. Today Magda and Elma, speaking of, are coming. Thank gourd!

Sunday. Darnell unhooked the receiver of the pay phone in the hall and it just dangled there all morning, a quiet threat. You could pulp someone's head with that thing. Then we took turns calling 911 from it. Heeeelp! we yowled. They're keeping us captive, feeding us drugs! Lola did a British accent. *Ah, yes, there's quite the uh-mah-gen-cy he-ah. It, ah, seems everyone's gone bah-nah-nahs.* We can't be held responsible for pranking 911. We're mental patients. When Dr. Garbian stepped into the hall, Micki was beatboxing for the operator. Hi, the rest of us said, waving, shuffling into a wall formation around Micki. He's on the phone with his father in Albania. We saluted, smiling at Dr. Garbian. Pu-puh-puh-chh pu-puh-puh-chh, Micki spit behind us, nodding feverishly. Dr. Garbian nodded, punched a code into the door, and disappeared into the courtyard.

Sundays are the best. Pancakes, movie night (*Pee-wee's Big Adventure*, what a neuter), no groups. Best of all, we get to go outside. We're albino creatures, atrophied muscles stretching painfully in the sun, faces turning up like tender leaves to the warm sky. Before I got here, Lola says, a girl hopped the fence. They called her Danzig because she had limp hair that she dyed black, she was from Jersey, and all she did was work out and wear her leather jacket around. She had a face like a seven-pound can of beans. I dunno. The fence is ten feet high and has iron rods sharpened to points at the top that curve in to disembowel you. I watched Danzig climb up fist over fist, Lola said. All that working out. When she landed on the other side, her boots shattered the sidewalk. Sonic boom.

Friday I was a lump. But not today. Today I feel effervescent, like I could float up into the sky. Even Micki won me over with his 911 beatboxing. Kind of. Not really. I feel bad for throwing his toothbrush into the trash. Now he has to use a state-issued one with a flexible handle. The bristles come off and get stuck in his teeth. He spends all morning pulling them out. So annoying. Now he'll have either bad breath from not brushing or state bristles in his teeth when he makes out with Lola in the middle of the night. She even wrote his name on the doorjamb. Someone penciled SUCKS under his name. Wasn't me, promise. I don't feel bad for Lola's boyfriend. It's like people can do whatever they want to us, but we're forced to adhere to a one-sided honor code? Make no mistake. We can do anything we want, just like them.

Today Lola braided my hair. She can't braid hers, because it's falling out. Brown strands litter the floor around her like piles of curled potato peelings. She has brown hair, brown teeth, brown eyes, brown skin. She is up to seventy-eight pounds now and pissed to be. She kept yanking my hair, pulling it, cursing. What? I said. I was nervous. What's going on up there? Nothing, nothing. When she was done, I looked in the mirror. I didn't know who that person was, half boy, half alien. You never had braids before? Lola pulled on the stiff sticks. They were like long leeches stuck to my head, sucking my brains. It hurts, I cried. Get used to it. So maybe that's why I feel hyperaware today. The tightly woven braids are doing something to me. Soon euphoria replaced the initial pain. Taut scalp equals euphoria. Who knew? I appreciate the way it feels, but it looks like shit. Lola's hands didn't stop shaking for a second when she was braiding. Every single braid is skinny in some places, fat in others, with lumps everywhere like little tumors and hair sticking out. I'm the poster girl for the mental hospital.

The euphoria could also be a remainder of Elma and Magda's visit yesterday. Actually, I think they made me more sad than happy, so that might not be true. I'm an ungrateful brat for saying that. My two closest friends, who drove out here to sit on the pee-stained couch for thirty minutes while trying to pretend the kids who didn't get visitors weren't pacing around the common room making fart sounds. Me, who shuffles around in tennis shoes with no laces and folds the waistband of her corduroys over three times because here a belt and shoelaces are also ways to get out.

The news from Magda and Elma is that Doug went missing after a rave in the desert. Moontribe. The time I dropped acid with him and left in the middle of it. I didn't understand why he was so upset. I just wanted to do something else, without him. Bye, I said, waving from Magda's cousin's car as he stood outside the coffee shop with his hands in his pockets. That was the night my mother drove to his house and dragged his grandma out of bed to search for me. I know she's here, my mother said, glaring. Doug followed them, holograms trailing incandescent copies of their bodies down the hallways, as the two women went around looking under beds and in closets, calling my name. It's so embarrassing I can't even stand to think about it. The next day he gave me a note he'd written after he got home.

Why did you leave? I walked for an hour up the hill. I saw an alien sitting in a tree. I asked it how old it was. I asked it what it had seen. I'll tell you in person. Why did you leave? I am smoking a beedi, drawing you, the alien that is my spirit animal.

Doug's great at drawing. He wants to be a graphic designer. What about me? No future. Where did I read that?

Elma and Magda got matching mini backpacks. You should get one, too, they said, but I could tell it was already their thing and they said that only because they felt bad for me. I'm not like them. I'm a freak. I don't have a father. Even though Magda's parents are divorced she still sees her dad all the time. He buys her clothes and takes her to sushi dinners. Elma and Magda always make plans together and then invite me later. What I really think is that they hate me. But then

I don't get why they even talk to me at all. I guess I can be kind of funny sometimes. Not really. I don't know. I wonder what they think of me in here, if they think I really tried to kill myself. Because I didn't.

Tuesday. Insomnia. Guess what. They caught Danzig and brought her back. She has scabs all over her face. She went straight to bed. Micki says she has some disease from her uncle, transmitted to her sexually. See why I hate him? He gossips. He makes up lies. How would he feel if I wrote *Micki has anal worms and pubic lice* under his name on the doorjamb? Maybe I will. I think Danzig tweeked out and tried to rip off her own face. Okay, I admit I'm relieved she's not in my and Lola's room, but it's not because I'm afraid of her face. It's because then it would ruin my thing with Lola. Me and Lola, who will walk into the world with steel arms linked, who will fell anybody in our way. What we both really want is just to be happy. When she's depressed, I'm depressed. When I'm hyper, she's hyper. We are two bruises on the same body. Last night, Lola couldn't sleep so we stayed up singing all the lyrics to Misfits songs as an ode to Danzig, a spell that would make her better. The skin on Lola's body is so thin you could slash it with a harsh word. She's at seventy-six today. Every pound is a lurid beast chasing her off a cliff. To see her sitting upright in bed is to see a corpse awaken. If she told me she wanted to die, I wouldn't argue. Because a body can do with itself what it wants. She didn't go across the hall to see Micki last night. Tank Man was on night watch. I've seen him pin down an eight-year-old kid and pull his arms so far behind him they cracked. I heard it. Tank Man will roll over anything in his way.

Thursday.

- A photo of me at Yosemite. Everyone else is smiling. I look like I'm about to cry. My sweatshirt is all dirty like I rolled around in dirt. My bangs are crooked and way too short, like my haircut is a joke to make everyone laugh. It's my fault. As a punishment, my mother gave me a choice: either cut an inch off my bangs or no reading for a week. She knows how much I love to read books. I can do without hair. Take it. I see myself in this photo and I'm disgusted. Like, *Get it together*.

- My mother has an inverted nipple. I used to lie on her chest and squeeze it until it got hard and poked out, like a little animal popping out of its lair.

- Being the only Asian here. The only Chinese girl.

- My father said that since his and my mother's families both immigrated to Taiwan from Mainland China, they're not really Taiwanese. What about me? I asked. You look Chinese but you're not. You're American.

- Playing with the golden retriever while my mother changed the old lady's diapers, washed her floors, and mopped up dog diarrhea. The dog's name was Tuna.

- All the kids in third grade had T-shirts that changed color, while my mother made me wear lace dresses to school.

- My sister dangled me by my arm out the window of our second-story townhouse at age four, telling me she was going to let go. I swung like a monkey.

A teenage boy was on the Superman ride at an amusement park when a taut cord snapped and whipped his legs, amputating both of them at the knee, the *LA Times* reports. The news is a hallucination.

I'm sitting at a small circular table writing, the pepper tree in the courtyard scattering sunlight all over these pages. The only window we can see clearly out of faces inward to the courtyard. There is nothing beyond what is visible to us. The cafeteria, our bedrooms, the showers, the office, the nurses' station, Dr. Garbian's office, the common room, the group therapy den with the word HONESTY stenciled on the door. An antiseptic medical smell permeates everything. The showers are blue-tiled, with high ceilings, how I remember the Hearst Castle pool, where I went with my mother once and we ate honey sticks from the gift shop afterward, licking our palms with sugared tongues. There's even an old nurse who sits in the showers while we wash our bodies, because it could be anytime, anywhere. A red button like a big mushroom sprouts from the wall amid the tiles. This mushroom sprouts from a wall in every room. I told you. Anytime. Anywhere.

Friday. So today I've been here for three and a half weeks. I'm infantilized. Wake now. Eat this. Swallow that. Talk about this. No, no. Bad girl. What's next? I shit myself, like the girl who was here for only one day, defecating black charcoal in her bed after getting her stomach pumped. She woke up thinking she had died, mistaking the nurses for angels in white scrubs. Typical. I guess she thought highly enough of herself to believe she was in heaven. She was a model. Took every pill she could find; guess they weren't the right kinds. They transferred her to a place in Malibu after her dad came with his credit card and the hospital figured out she wasn't on low-income federal insurance like the rest of us. When am I getting out? Joley got out. Cordy got out. Micki got out. That's the good thing that happened this week. I dunked his high-tops in the toilet as a going-away present but he didn't even care. The one body who will never get out is Darnell. They say he's been here for six months. So what if he gets angry a lot. If you had to go through what he goes through, you'd be much angrier than he is. You'd have flames shooting from your back. Group home, mental hospital, juvie. This is our circuit. We are runaways, drug addicts, dangers to ourselves and others. We need help. Help us. In the bathroom today there were tiny brown flakes all over the white porcelain sink. I didn't realize what they were until I saw Danzig in the cafeteria with her face all bleeding and raw.

Last night Lola told me about the first time she did heroin. Her mother was high, screaming at her for ruining her life. Lola said, I took the needle that had just been inside her body and stuck it in mine. All those years watching her do it. It was as if I had always done it. I did it because I was so mad at her I didn't know what else to do. Then Lola and I fell asleep in the same bed, dreaming about our mothers.

In family group today they asked me to start. What changes would you like your family to make in order to help you get better? What family? It's just my mother. I want her to leave me alone, I said, pulling my legs up to my chin. I mean, sure, I want that, but what am I supposed to say? That I would like to have a father. That I would like to have a sister who had never locked me in the garage for two days when my mother was out of town, my six-year-old self snapping spiderwebs with my face as I ambled around in the darkness. That my sister wasn't married to such a creep. That I would like a normal mother, a mother who doesn't get so mad she digs her fingernails into my face, carving red crescent moons in my cheeks, who didn't leave me at the mall at age seven and drive home by herself because I took too long smelling erasers in the stationery store, who doesn't say things like: Why don't you just kill yourself, then? And: All I want is to die! Because I want to show her that I can do anything. I can do anything she wants me to do. There are two different languages, a language you speak out loud to others, and a language that can never be spoken.

Across the circle of chairs my mother sits, hating me. She hates me for piercing my tongue. She hates me for talking on the phone. She hates me for so many things, but why does she really hate me? Coughing, wheezing, even her body hates me. I know why she hates me. For the same reason my sister hates me. Because I am my father's daughter. The devil's spawn. But you know what? I hate him too. I'm on their side. They don't get it, though.

My mother points at me from the opposite side of the circle. There is something wrong with her, she says. She is not normal. Only bad person like this. Chinese girl not like this. Well, I am a Chinese girl and I am exactly like this.

So I get bad grades. So I shaved the back of my head. So I smoked pot a few times. So I got drunk and had sex once. So I snuck out the window to go to a party. So she told me to go kill myself for the hundredth time and I scratched up my arms with a dull box cutter. So what.

Monday. If I've learned anything in life, it's to always be prepared for the earth beneath me to open up. I can never grow wings, but I've learned to face the plummet. When Lola told me she was getting out, she might as well have reached into my body and yanked out my spine, taking with it all the other bones it was attached to. The rest of me pooled on the hospital linoleum. Back to the group home Tuesday morning and then hopefully, soon, to live with her mom again. Why is it that there is no place more hellish than home, yet there is no other place we'd rather return to? If it doesn't work out, she'll run away with her boyfriend, or Micki. Why don't you run away with me? I asked, but she just said Yeah and kept putting her clothes into a nylon bag. I can't even write anymore. What's the point.

Sunday. So much has happened. Where do I begin? I'm still here. Before Lola left, she got down to seventy-three pounds in anticipation of reentry into the real world. Why did they decide to let you out and not me? I asked her. You've lost weight since you've been here. Lola grabbed my arms and turned them over, then back again. Superficial, she said, rubbing her hand up and down my arms. Any fool can see this is not a legitimate suicide attempt. You know why I'm getting out? Why? I asked. 'Cause my insurance ran out. You know why you're still here? I shook my head. Because my insurance didn't run out? Lola cupped my chin with one hand. No, baby. Because your mama doesn't want you to get out.

Two weeks into my stay, they wanted to release me, but my mother refused my homecoming. During Lola's daily visits to the nurse to get weighed and have her vitals taken, she overheard my mother on speakerphone with Dr. Garbian in the next room. She is out of control! There is no improvement. I am afraid of her. I cannot take responsibility when she goes crazy again. No way. If you release her, I will not be there. I will not pick her up.

I stare at Lola as she tells me this, her cracked lips oiled with apricot gloss, searching for deceit in her countenance. There's something in her voice that makes me wonder if she's lying to spare me the truth. The truth that I'm here because there really is something very, very wrong with me.

The last night Lola was here we slept in the same bed, curled around each other like a compound word. Remember that dream you had where you found the journal of the missing girl with the words *Wound Bound* written in it? she asked. The way her breath smells after she throws up. I'll even miss that. I nodded, burying my face in her shoulder. I've been thinking about that, Lola said. We considered the homonyms, the doubling, each permutation of the two words circling our bed. *Wound Bound.* In the morning, standing by the office next to her bags, I gave her my silver neck-lace, a small fava bean on a slender chain. It was still warm when I fastened it around her neck, the bean nestled between her collarbones. I've never had this with anybody. Not even Magda or Elma. Lola's the only one who understands. I watched a woman with long dreadlocks hug her, lift her bags, take her away down the winding courtyard path into the main hospital building. I know I'll never see her again.

Doug called on the pay phone. Where are you? I asked. Nowhere, he said.

Me too.

wound (noun)

1. an injury to the body

2. an emotional injury

wound (transitive and intransitive verb)

1. to injure

2. to cause an emotional wound

wound (past participle, past tense of *wind*)

bound (past participle, past tense of *bind*)

bound (adjective)

1. certain to do something

2. obligated

3. determined

bound (intransitive verb)

1. to move quickly and energetically, with large strides or jumps

bound (adjective)

1. on one's way somewhere

2. destined

bound (transitive verb)

1. to surround an area

2. to restrict something

bound (noun)

1. a limiting number

bound (adjective)

1. not constituting a word
2. not constituting a sentence

Tuesday. My father came today. It's not even visiting day. They made an exception for him. Why are they always making exceptions for fathers? He sat across the table from me. Why are you doing this to yourself? Why do you not behave for your mother? She says you have lost your mind. I know you are a smart girl. Oh yeah, how the hell does he know that? He doesn't even know me. He doesn't know anything about me. Since the age of six, I have seen this motherfucker once a year, tops, and that's if I'm lucky. Tell me, he says. I am your father. How can I ever tell him? All I can do is sit there and cry. Not a word.

Friday. There's a killer on the loose today. A former military sniper has been stalking victims in Reseda, Montebello, San Pedro, taking them out one by one. You are not safe even in your own house. No one knows where he will strike next. It's on every page of the newspaper. The motive, they say, is vengeance.

In the womb, the umbilical cord wrapped around my neck. My mother and I. Our two hearts stopped beating. You almost killed me, she said, brushing my hair back with a sideways hand.

My sister told me that when she was little, she used to sit on the windowsill and blow bubbles into the street, wishing they would go out into the world and bring my mother back.

Before I was born, after my mother divorced my sister's father, she would go out on dates all night with my father, leaving my sister home by herself. In Taiwan, maybe this is not illegal.

Saturday. Today they found Danzig hanging from the shower.

Sunday. Once, I was so mad at my mother I peed in her soup. Once, I was so mad at my mother I cut my arms. Once, I was so mad at my mother I penetrated her with my penis in a dream. I don't want to feel alone anymore. I am alone so much. I wish there was a door accessible at all times, from anywhere, a room I can enter and find my mother sitting in. Anytime. Anywhere. Every time I remember something new about my childhood, I will open the door and tell her. Every time I think about something awful she's said, I will open the door and yell at her. Every time I want to ask her questions about my father, I will open the door and ask her. Every time

I want to hear a story, I will open the door and listen. I can go in and say, *I am sad right now, Mother. I am lonely right now, Mother. I am angry right now, Mother.* See, it isn't about the father. It is the mother. It is always my mother. Everything I do, everything I am, it is her. I have nothing in this world except for my mother. I am so mad at my mother.

PLEASE FORGIVE ME, PELE

by Ryan Thompson

INTRODUCTION

The following pages document a number of volcanic rocks and other objects that were taken from, and returned to, Hawaii, alongside a selection of apology letters from the archives at Haleakala and Hawaii Volcanoes National Parks. Some letter writers acknowledge an apocryphal story of a curse wrought by Pele, the Hawaiian goddess of volcanoes and fire, on anyone who removes volcanic rocks from Hawaii. Others simply express feelings of remorse or a desire to return something that was not theirs to take.

Maybe this phenomenon is evidence of a common human folly, rooted in a worldview that regards the landscape as little more than a source of touristic curios. On the other hand, these small acts of repatriation represent a desire for redemption, liberation, and justice. I see both perspectives reflected simultaneously in these objects but prefer to emphasize the latter. Doing so, I believe, has the potential to help us reimagine our relationship to this place—to *any*place—and to its people, and to glimpse a flicker of Hawaiian sovereignty right in front of us.

If not for volcanic eruptions spanning millions of years, the islands of Hawaii would not exist. If not for colonialism, Hawaii would still be a sovereign nation. If not for the whims of tourists (myself included), we would not be here reading these letters and looking at these photographs. Yet here we find ourselves, full of hubris, hopefully learning something, so we can make better mistakes tomorrow.

—Ryan Thompson

WE ARE VERY SORRY
THAT WE TOOK THE SAND
OUR LIVES HAVE BEEN
A LIVING HELL SINCE
WE TOOK IT.

PLEASE RE-
TURN TO
HAWAII'S
EARTH.
THANK YOU

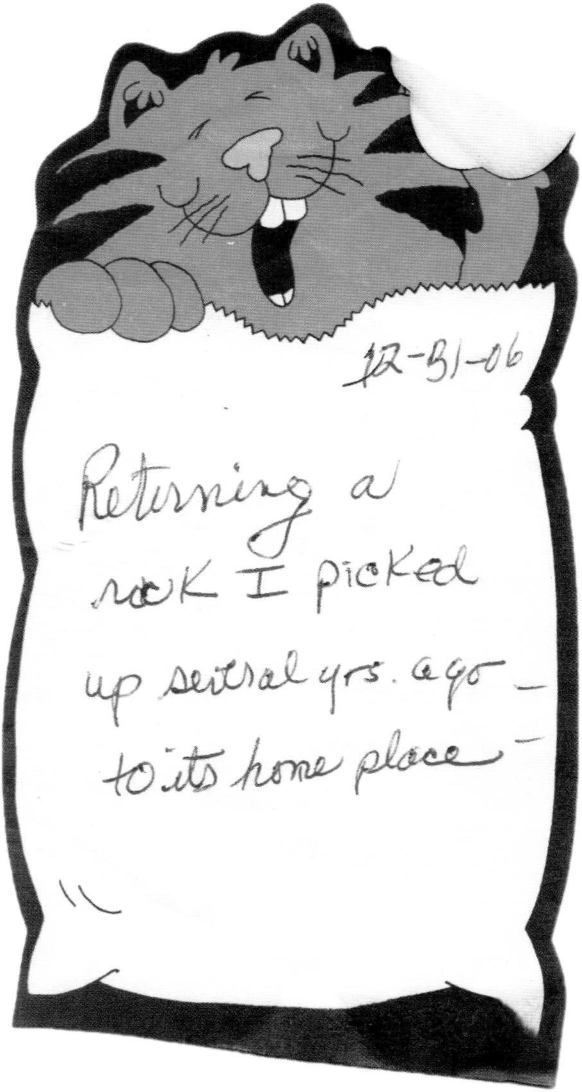
12-31-06
Returning a rock I picked up several yrs. ago – to its home place –

These were taken
during my Honeymoon
in October 1994.

Sorry!

The inside
Hawai'i Volcanoes National park

My uncle bought this in Hawai'i

approximately 40 years ago.

I return this to Pele,

and, Please do it.

Aloha Rangers,   11/30/06

   Found these ROCKS AT A GARAGE SALE IN OMAHA NEBRASKA YEARS AGO.

   TIRED OF ALL THE BAD LUCK AND JUSTIFICATIONS THAT COME WITH IT.

   PLEASE GENTLY RETURN THESE TO MADAME PELE.

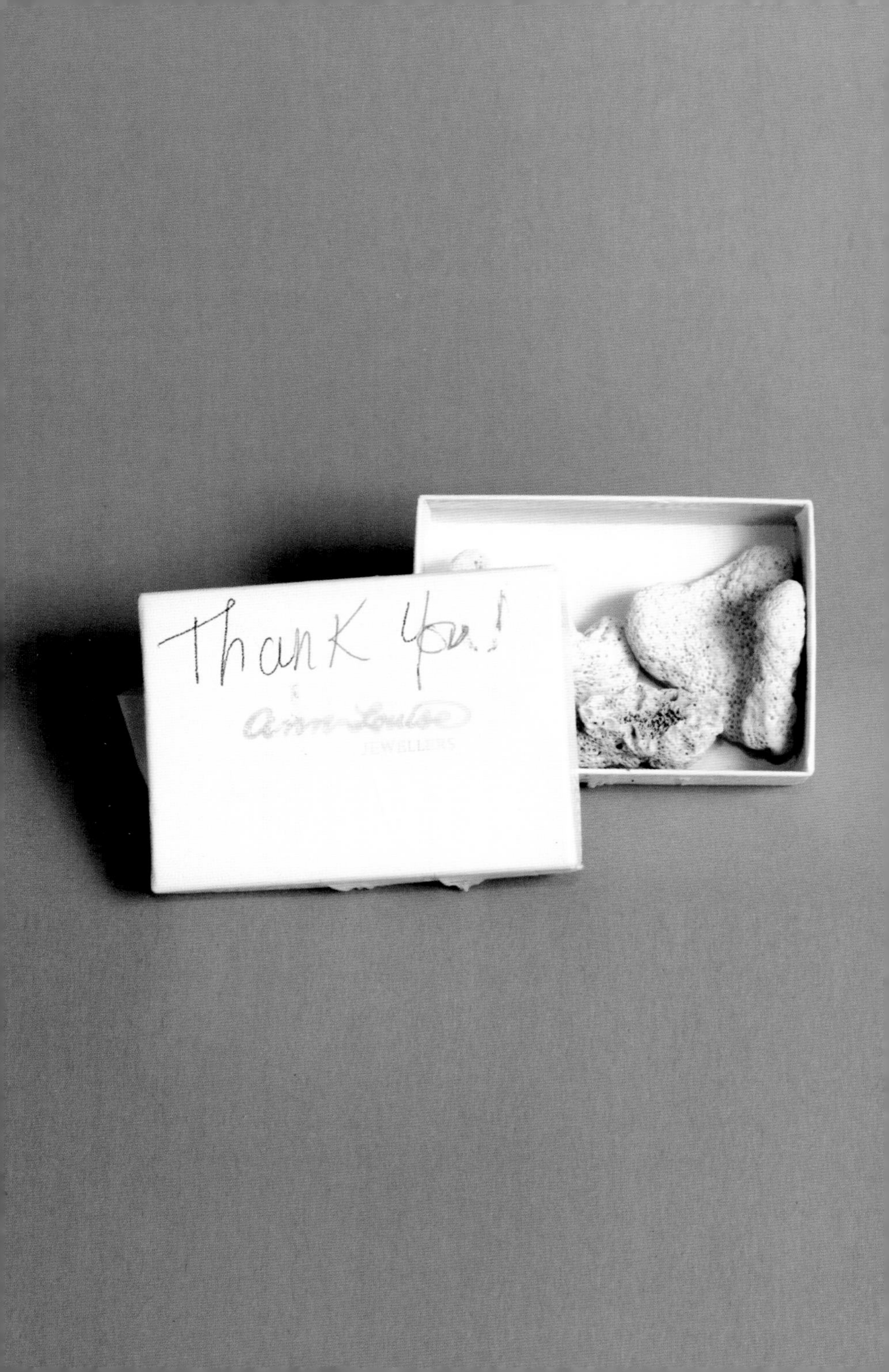
Thank You!
JEWELLERS

Everybody Wins!
Lottery dollars support education and
other vital programs in Washington.

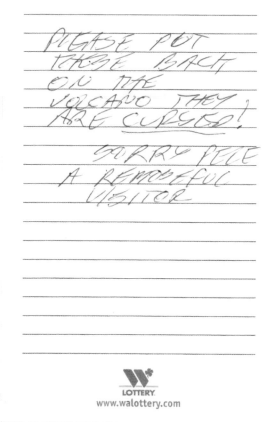

PLEASE PUT
THESE BACK
ON THE
VOLCANO THEY
ARE CURSED!

SORRY PETE
A REMORSEFUL
VISITOR

Please accept the tennis shoes that I wore on Kilauea during our shore visit from the Norwegian Cruise Line. My luck has not been very good since I have been home. I was not a wise visitor to the volcano and I apologize. I should have left a gift.
I'm sorry

(scratt marks & rock)

Any lava possibly left on my shoes belong back on Kilauea. Thank you.

BAD MOJO

PLEASE RETURN TO
CHAIN OF CRATERS ROAD
LAVA FLOW

THANKS

Please Forgive Me Pele

MAY 2017

10/2/03

Dear Pete:

Please accept our apologies for removing
the included rock from your island. We
are sincerely sorry, and are hopeful this
gesture will reverse our fortunes.

On behalf of my family with regrets,

Please say "I'm sorry"
for God of Volcano.

Thank You.

I humbly beg your
forgiveness.

me.

CONSPIRATORS'
NOTES

by EDWARD GAUVIN

Someday we must write the history of our own obscurity—manifest the density of our narcissism, tally down through the centuries the several appeals to difference we may have occasionally heard, the ideological recuperations which have infallibly followed and which consist in always acclimating our incognizance of Asia by means of certain known languages...

—Roland Barthes, *Empire of Signs*, trans. Richard Howard

EDWARD GAUVIN is a translator from the French. A full-time freelancer since 2006, he has made a living from almost exclusively creative work in various fields, from film to fiction, with a personal focus on contemporary comics (bande-dessinée) and post-Surrealist literatures of the fantastic. His translations have appeared in the *New York Times*, *Harper's Magazine*, the *Guardian*, and *World Literature*

Today, and have twice placed—first and second—in the British Comparative Literature Association's John Dryden Translation Competition. They have also been shortlisted for the Oxford-Weidenfeld Prize, the Albertine Prize, the Best Translated Book Award, the National Translation Award, and have twice been nominated for the French-American Foundation's Translation Prize. He has received fellowships and residencies from the Guggenheim Foundation, the National Endowment for the Arts, PEN America, Ledig House, the Lannan Foundation, the Banff Centre, and the French and Belgian governments.

EDWARD GAUVIN is a nom de plume.

EDWARD GAUVIN was born in Hanoi, where his Vietnamese mother was raised and his father, a French diplomat, was stationed. His isn't a face you'd think of as mixed, but then again, that isn't a thing you'd think to ask. Not, at any rate, with that face officially subtitled by a name tag at a convention hotel bar, the very kind of venue where Gauvin and an editor friend, cackling at the chance for some literary skullduggery, devised this backstory over copious drinks. "In the face of the inexplicable," writes Kevin Young in *Bunk*, "audiences will settle for unbelievable." A pen name, you say? Pen names are taken left and right, as prerogative or prerequisite, for privacy or protection, in probity or in prank. Cui malo? And you'd be right, had Edward Gauvin not signed contracts, cashed checks, married, and figured in that Great American Novel we all write, our Collected Federal Income Tax Returns, in whose minutiae—deductions, joint filings, claimed dependents—the details of a life are adumbrated. As an artist, to change your name is to come into your own. As an American, it is a matter of birthright. Eventually, Edward Gauvin "produced a body," attending literary events where he is often asked, "Hey, aren't you that guy who does comics?"

GEORGE PSALMANAZAR (c. 1679–1763) rates a passing mention from Jonathan Swift, who adduces to his *Modest Proposal* the former's testimony that natives of the island of Formosa, like himself, consume youths sacrificed by the thousands in a tabernacle to an ox god. Psalmanazar details this ritual in his book *A Historical and Geographical Description of Formosa* (1704), right down to "the Gridiron upon which the hearts of the young Children are burnt." Formosans, he claims, broke their fasts by sucking the blood from freshly beheaded vipers, and sported animal hides or kimonos left open to flaunt posing-pouches of bark, for the lower classes, and precious metals, for the upper, who preserved the pallor of skin, like his own, by living underground—as he was aware that "my complexion, indeed, which was very fair, appeared an unanswerable objection against" the claims he made for his origin. Blond, blue-eyed, and by most belated biographical accounts a Frenchman, Salmanaazor, or Salamanzer—his name, said to be shared with the ox god's prophet, sometimes contained as many as six *a*'s and may have been inspired by the biblical monarch Shalmaneser—delighted the dinner tables of England for several decades with such displays of foreignness as feasting on raw meat. When challenged at the Royal Society, he took care to distinguish "Formosa, an Island subject to the Emperor of Japan," in whose capital city of Xternetsa he had been born, from "Tyowan," a different island, colonized by the Dutch, which he claimed people from China referred to as "Pak-Ando," and which Formosans called "Gad-Avia." Psalmanazar fabricated a Formosan language, with which he produced "translations" of the Anglican catechism, and his factitious alphabet was found in language manuals well beyond his lifetime.

Wordplay is what most people I meet assume comics abound in, so—fittingly, perhaps—my interest in it dates from a young age. Autumn sun warmed the lobby where, among the kids of band and orchestra waiting for their parents, I was first called a "chink." To which I replied, "A chink off the old block!" It is hard to say who was more nonplussed: the drummer in his Mötley Crüe tee, which had earned him a visit to the vice principal, or the second violinist, who, deducing an insult but not its nature, snowcloned from his reading of *The Hardy Boys* a phrase he suspected was a compliment. Call it an alliterative lark. Call it, after Adrienne Rich, "(the fracture of order / the repair of speech / to overcome this suffering)." Haven't you heard? They burn paper now, not children, not even their ears. Sticks and stones are sounds before they're substance.

Perhaps you've heard this one before. A foreign writer, basking in the twilit warmth of a long-overdue if still minor American tour, visits a small northeastern women's college, where an admiring student presses on him a translation of what time seems to have anointed as his finest work, composed at the height of his artistic potency. One torrid night later, he leaves her with a novel and a child, whom she raises on his belatedly growing reputation in the States and royalties from the publication of her manuscript (that's how you know this is a fable). Once grown, the child makes his way to his father's homeland with many questions. Who is that young man, asking about the late, great author? He speaks his father's language with an accent, but he has his father's eyes. Is this a metaphor or a memoir? Yes.

A chevalier de la Légion d'Honneur, fabulist GEORGES-OLIVIER CHÂTEAUREYNAUD (1947–) won the Prix des Nouvelles Littéraires with his second book, the Kafkaesque novella *Les messagers*. For the next decade, he cobbled together a living as a cashier, a truck driver, an antiques dealer, and a librarian before winning the Prix Renaudot, on whose jury he has served ever since. Over a career of twelve novels (including two under an alias), two memoirs, and more than one hundred short stories, he has been awarded the Prix Goncourt for short fiction, the Grand Prix de l'Imaginaire from the international festival of science fiction and fantasy Utopiales, and the Prix Louis Barthou from the Académie française for his body of work, translated into over fifteen languages before finally making its way into English. Along with novelist Hubert Haddad and two fellow Goncourt winners, businessman Frédérick Tristan and sinologist Jean Lévi, Châteaureynaud is a founding member of the contemporary movement La nouvelle fiction: "new" because it rose up against the prevailingly minimalist and confessional tendencies of autofiction, seeking to rouse recent French letters from what critic Jean-Luc Moreau called "the slumber of psychological realism," restoring myth, fable, and fairy tale to a place of primacy in fiction.

THOMAS CORAGHESSAN, or T. C. BOYLE (1948–), born Thomas John Boyle, won the PEN/Faulkner Award in 1988 for his third novel, *World's End*, and the Prix Médicis Étranger for his sixth, *The Tortilla Curtain*. He is the author of eighteen novels and more than one hundred short stories, which have been anthologized in multiple volumes of *The Best American Short Stories* and have been honored with the Rea Award, the National Magazine Award, the O. Henry Award, the Bernard Malamud Prize in Short Fiction, and the PEN Center West Literary Prize. He has received fellowships from the National

Endowment for the Arts and the Guggenheim Foundation. At a conference on short fiction in the late 1980s, Boyle— who had penned stories in which Lassie, in heat, leaves Timmy to die; a primatologist quits her live-in boyfriend for an ape; and blood rains down from the skies—stood up, in his customary black leather jacket and red Converse high-tops, to a panel of Dirty Realists then presiding aesthetically over the American short story and, addressing his fellow Iowa alum Raymond Carver, said, "Not all of us do it your way, Ray, and there's got to be room for that."

EDWARD GAUVIN has translated more than four hundred graphic novels for such publishers as Top Shelf, SelfMadeHero, IDW, BOOM! Studios, Lerner Graphic Universe, Magnetic Press, Uncivilized Books, NBM, First Second, and Europe Comics. His work on books by such creators as Marjane Satrapi, Alejandro Jodorowsky, Claire Bretécher, Li Kunwu, Christophe Blain, David B., Blutch, Edmond Baudoin, Frederik Peeters, Nie Jun, and Zeina Abirached has received over twenty Eisner Award nominations and two Batchelder Award Honors from the American Library Association. From 2016 to 2018, he cohosted a monthly episode on European comics with the late Dr. Derek Royal for *The Comics Alternative* podcast. With artist Claire Stephens, he has published short comics on the paradoxes of translation in the *Arkansas International* and *Words without Borders*, where he is a contributing editor for comics. He has spoken on

Francophone *bande-dessinée* at universities, festivals, and cons, where people will say, if they say anything at all, "Didn't you do some science fiction once?"

While a student at Harvard, ROBERT DUNN (1916–83) of Somerville, Massachusetts, won a 1936 essay contest sponsored by New York City's Ging Hawk Club, an organization for young, mostly college-educated, American-born Chinese women. In response to the prompt "Does My Future Lie in China or America?," Dunn deemed that securing remunerative employment, though difficult, was not impossible in America, and advocated staying here to build up "a good impression of the Chinese among Americans," believing that by doing so he might forestall for himself "unhappiness and social estrangement due to conflicting cultures." The *Chinese Digest*, the first continental English-language newspaper, founded as an engine of assimilation for second-generation Chinese Americans, printed his winning entry, provoking an open letter from the Stanford University Chinese Students' Club that lambasted Dunn for "fallacies in reasoning," "ignorance of China's needs," "misconceptions of Chinese culture and civilization," and a "biased viewpoint" that was "pathetic and misleading," clearly that of "an unsympathetic American who has never lived in China. You judge China by American standards—political, economic, and moral." To Dunn's musings on the feasibility of employment, the letter riposted, "What fanciful illusions of equality were you

dreaming about? If not the 'color line'—the racial preju-
dice—what is keeping Chinese out of American industries
and governmental offices? Surely not the lack of ability."

H. V. CHAO (2009–) has published short fiction in the *Kenyon
Review*, *West Branch*, *Birkensnake*, and the *Saturday Evening
Post*. His work has also been translated by A.-S. Homassel
in *Le visage vert* and *Angle mort*. To falsify one parent hints
at estrangement; to falsify both smacks of premeditation.
Gauvin adopted his mother's maiden name in honor of the
woman who raised him and his brother. "There was nothing
unusual in the appearance" of Chao, and his "knowledge of
physics was moderate," but "actually he had one distinction
that is rarely encountered—he was born at the age of twenty-five and entered the world with a memory but without
a personal experience to account for it," as was first asserted
of Mr. John Furriskey, a character in a novel within Flann
O'Brien's novel *At Swim-Two-Birds*, which takes disingenuous
pains to disclaim, "All the characters represented, including
the first person singular, are entirely fictitious." Chao made
his debut in the pages of the literary magazine *Epiphany* with
the story "Jewel of the North," in which a mysterious snow-
fall afflicting a small lakeside resort off-season is revealed to
be the ashes of bureaucratic paperwork, borne on the wind
from burning archives in the distant, sacked capital.

* * *

EDWARD GAUVIN is the winner of the inaugural Science Fiction and Fantasy Translation Award. He spent a year as a Fulbright Scholar in Brussels, studying the Francophone tradition of supernatural fiction known as the Belgian School of the Bizarre. A contributor to Rachel S. Cordasco's history *Out of This World: Speculative Fiction in Translation from the Cold War to the New Millennium*, he wrote a regular column for Ann and Jeff VanderMeer's *Weird Fiction Review* profiling post-Surrealist French fantastical writers, several of whom he went on to resurrect or debut in English, with translations appearing in *Fantasy & Science Fiction*, *Asimov's Science Fiction*, *Podcastle*, and *Conjunctions*. When he attends science fiction and fantasy conventions, people sometimes say: "So... you're a translator?"

Once, at just such a con, EDWARD GAUVIN sat bemoaning, to a science fiction writer, his various hats and how he never seemed to be wearing the right one at the right time. "But that's what makes you so interesting!" the writer exclaimed. He was white, of course, and could contain multitudes. Whereas Gauvin had always experienced being any one thing as belying, if not betraying, another. The writer's encouragements recalled how certain commiserations—"Those are good problems to have," or "You'll be fine!"—had always felt to him, in his disconsolate precocity, more like kiss-offs. It is a genuine, if minor, predicament to feel ungrateful for what is well-intentioned, like being a friend no one ever knows how to shop for. Or an Asian American applauded for diligence. If wearing many hats is so interesting, he thought but did not say, then why do I feel so lonely?

EDWARD GAUVIN has moved—for love, work, or study—an average of every two years since he turned eighteen, living in Los Angeles, Austin, Pittsburgh, Newark, Manhattan, Amiens, Taipei, San Jose, Eugene, and Sacramento, among others. On paper, this list comes off as cosmopolitan, like he might suavely, savvily pronounce on eateries, nightlife, or local custom, but on balance, he spent most of his time feeling ambiently judged and excluded, uselessly agonizing over whether to go out, and once out, hurrying home past lighted windows to rooms affordably remote from the lively city center, where he pored over maps, exhaustively plotting solitary travels of devout punctuality. He never has a good answer to which of all the places he's lived he likes best. They were all the same, in that he moved on. He blended in but never really belonged. When he revisits a place, he feels as much a stranger as ever—one who somehow knows what subway car to ride for which exit, or what freeway lane to be in for which off-ramp.

That autumn afternoon, the fourth-grade drummer, who shared a surname (no relation) with the pizza franchise soon to open in the food court at the new mall, retorted, "Yeah, well, that's your old block, stay away from mine." Which, for me, cleared up nothing. Children of the internet, forgive me. Idiom was vaporous as rumor then. Whom could you ask about what everyone knew without letting on that you didn't? A predicament common to espionage and precocity. Long after fleeing the parentally imposed strings—*pity the wood that finds itself a violin*—I persisted, for instance, in my homophony of *eligible* and *illegible* until chagrined by a college girlfriend's laughter. Criticism comes from love, my mother chided; what stranger would bother? Yet how many were the questions she couldn't answer... I can't remember now when I found out what a "chink" was, much less an "old block"; it was later still before I fit the two together with that afternoon, which came to seem, despite the shedding of new light, a little more occluded. The old block has been on my shoulder ever since.

Artist, landscape architect, theatrical and industrial designer ISAMU NOGUCHI (1904–88) was born in the United States but spent his childhood in Japan. He first returned to America at fourteen for Interlaken, a boarding school adrift on the Indiana plains, whose students, living in log cabins they had built and off the land they themselves farmed, pursued, as per the school's motto, "Knowledge through Experience." According to his mother, Léonie Gilmour, who raised him, Noguchi was "inclined to admire all things American, and to slight his Japanese ancestry." Not until he dropped out of

Columbia College six years later did he shed the name Sam Gilmour to pursue sculpture full-time as Isamu Noguchi. Shortly thereafter, he received a Guggenheim Fellowship, which he spent studying in Paris and traveling through Asia. In the summer of 1941, he drove across America in a station wagon with a friend, lyrical abstractionist Arshile Gorky, who had fled the Armenian genocide, and whose troubled relationship with his own father had led him to take a new surname, claiming to be a Georgian noble related to the famous Russian writer. "Gorky felt that he wasn't totally American," Noguchi told Gorky's biographer. "I think he emphasized his non-Americanness... And there was a kind of bond between us, not being entirely American, you see. We were friends... and we had a certain loneliness here." Shortly after World War II, Gorky would hang himself, but the day the war began for America, Noguchi was driving south from Los Angeles to a stone supplier near San Diego in the same Ford station wagon. His first thought on hearing the breaking news on December 7, 1941, was "Oh my God, I'm a Japanese—or I'm a Nisei at least." And then: "I must do something. But first I had to get to know my fellow Nisei; I had previously no reason to seek them out as a group."

In November 2005, WORDS WITHOUT BORDERS (2003–) published Edward Gauvin's first translation, "Delaunay the Broker" by Georges-Olivier Châteaureynaud—a noted figure, along with Annie Saumont, Marie-Hélène Lafon, and Daniel

Boulanger, in the renaissance of French short fiction that had begun in the 1970s. Over the next three years, Gauvin went on to publish translations of eleven more stories by the same author in journals from the *Southern Review* to *AGNI* to *Harvard Review*, before approaching Gavin J. Grant and Kelly Link's Small Beer Press, a Massachusetts-based indie publisher devoted to literary speculative fiction, with a book proposal. (This was how Gauvin, a product of the MFA system, conceived of the path to publication.) The final manuscript, a volume of selected stories from eight collections, spanning four decades of Châteaureynaud's work, was published in 2010, taking its name from one of the stories: *A Life on Paper*.

"I think this invention," mused BRIAN O'NOLAN (1911–66), writing to the publisher of his pen name, Flann O'Brien, "has the advantage that it contains an unusual name and one that is quite ordinary." Edward, as we know from Robert Louis Stevenson, is the opposite of Henry. My parents, fearing they'd given me a first name too difficult for kindergarten mouths, told my teacher to call me Henry, and so it was in the year of being Henry that I starred as one of seven dwarves in a predominantly diminutive production of *Snow White*. The year after—elementary motor speech having, I suppose, made the grade—I assumed my given name, only a letter away from a common if passé English one, the kind of fusty, august, ex-presidential moniker so fragrant to Chinese immigrant parents. This inaugurated a childhood of magnanimous corrections from adults, which I met with disdain. After all, which of us had worn a burnt orange cardigan to the county spelling bee? My English was impeccable. Gauvin, on the other hand, is... close to the French for Gawain? My favorite Arthurian knight, I retconned for want of a more thrilling backstory, though he wasn't. (Did I even have one? To the tortured, self-flagellating Lancelot; the comically innocent Percival; the doomed lover Tristan; or even, in my more aspirational interludes, the impossibly pure Galahad, I could at least relate.) Neither my mother, her second husband (now ex-), nor my rural, white Michigan in-laws have ever gotten "Gauvin" right, out loud or on paper, and polite inquiries precede every panel and interview. Plus ça change... The irony is such that one might even think Edward Gauvin were simply nostalgic. "Also, reinforcing the idea of a self as a relational rather than an independent entity," footnotes Gish Jen in her Massey Lectures, "my father had at least two other Chinese names—a 'milk' name used by his parents and an everyday name used by his friends and schoolmates. He acquired an English name, Norman, as well, when he came to the United States, along with several nicknames, and never much cared what anyone called him, in any case."

THE CHINESE EXCLUSION ACT (1882), the first and only major federal legislation to deny a person's entry into the United States based upon ethnicity or country of birth, was conceived largely in response to fears that the "yellow peril" had become too prolific a source of cheap labor. It's a thin line between containing multitudes and being legion. Renewed by the Geary Act a decade later and made permanent in 1902, it effectively ended all Chinese immigration to United States for the next sixty years. In response to these "hundred kinds of oppressive laws," many Chinese resorted to falsifying paperwork that claimed blood relation to an existing American citizen, or membership in one of the classes exempt from exclusion: diplomats, teachers, students, merchants, travelers. As immigrant Ted Chan told historian Erika Lee in an interview, "If we told the truth, it didn't work. So we had to take the crooked path." A booming multinational business in forged documents arose, greatly abetted by the mass destruction of public birth records in the fire that raged across San Francisco for days after the devastating earthquake of 1906. It is estimated that 90 to 95 percent of Chinese immigrants who entered the United States during these decades did so as "paper sons"—a lie told, indeed tailored, in order to belong. Edward Gauvin has always looked good on paper.

For the purposes of this account, I will indulge a détournement of MICHEL FOUCAULT (1926–84), and, in asking "What is a translator?," pursue a sociohistorical analysis of Edward Gauvin as an individual and the numerous questions that deserve attention in this context: how the translator was individualized in a culture such as ours; the status we have given the translator, for instance, when we began our research into authenticity and attribution; the systems of valorization in which he was included; or the moment when the stories of traitors gave way to a translator's biography; the conditions that fostered the formulation of the fundamental critical category of "the man and his work." To learn, for example, that I was born not in Hanoi but Atlanta; that my mother, Helen Chao, was in fact born in China and raised in Taiwan; that my father was neither a diplomat nor Vietnamese, does not invalidate the fact that my name continues to refer to the same person; there has been no modification of the designation that links the name to the person. With Edward Gauvin, however, the problems are far more complex. The disclosure that Gauvin was born in the United States would not necessarily modify the functioning of the translator's name, but were it established that he was not hapa, this would constitute a change and affect the manner in which the translator's identity is perceived. Moreover, if we establish that Gauvin had no Vietnamese ancestry, inherited no trauma from the sordid French colonial history of Indochina or the United States' protracted entanglements there that undermined its vision of itself, we would have introduced a third type of alteration, which completely modifies the functioning of the translator's identity. Consequently, the name of this translator is not precisely a pseudonym among others. Some are born to a name, some choose their own, and some are told it doesn't matter that they aren't Japanese when their locker is desecrated for Pearl Harbor Day. We can conclude that, unlike a proper name, which moves from the interior of a discourse to the real person outside who produced it, the name of the translator remains at the contours of histories—separating one from the other, defining their form, and characterizing their mode of existence. All Asian Americans are alike, but every Asian American is Asian in their own way. Versions of Gauvin have proliferated, repeatedly revised for fear of being doubted or believed, but one element remains constant: his fascination with French stems from daddy issues, that relatable Freudian detail. For a long time, he resentfully eschewed the language of the father who'd left him at an early age, but eventually, curiosity about his heritage got the better of him. When he first moved to France, he hadn't even the words to buy a baguette, and though the years he spent living and teaching there cured him of this, he still speaks his father's language with an accent.

Hounded by accusations of how "poorly qualified" he was to opine on such topics, ROBERT DUNN confessed that in the initial draft of his prizewinning essay, he "immediately and instinctively chose the side favoring a future in China," but upon finding out that entries would be evaluated for their "originality of thought," switched sides, playing devil's advocate. In other words, the opinions expressed were not the author's own and did not reflect his beliefs—namely, that China was "really 'the line of least resistance' for young Chinese Americans." Shortly thereafter, Dunn moved to Chungking, where he worked in the Chinese civil service and, later, for the Chinese delegation to the United Nations. While in China, he began using his full name: Robert Dunn Wu.

Despite a notable lack of other Asians at my high school, I was not the valedictorian of my graduating class, to the surprise of many who thought they knew me. The long arc of disappointment that would divide me from my parents had begun sophomore year: AP Physics, subsequent discouragement, lack of application, musical theater. Still, great things were vaguely expected; rumor had it I would major in film. Commencement took place one muggy June evening on a football field in suburban New Jersey, the clouds massed for downpour. I waited in a folding chair on the fifty-yard line for my name to be mispronounced, recalling every garbled summons to the block at every varsity swim meet. These things do and don't matter. They add up and vanish, then all come back at once. Caps were tossed; from the bleachers, parents cheered. In the sparse rain just starting to wet our cheeks, EDWARD GAUVIN, class royalty, took me by the shoulders. "Promise me one thing," he said, his blue eyes bright. "Even after you make it big, promise, promise you'll never change your name."

THE FRENCH PUBLISHERS' AGENCY (1983–) is a boutique literary agency representing English-language rights "for a highly selective yet widely diverse list of books" from

publisher members of its umbrella organization, a cultural out-
reach arm funded by the French government. The year I spent
there as an agent—showing up always late and harried, in
ill-fitting clothes, to lunches at places I could otherwise never
have afforded—proved more an education in the basics of New
York socializing than a springboard to my subsequent free-
lancing career. It was the culmination of two years of mostly
temping, punctuated now and then by being fired from or
walking out on jobs where I was shocked to discover that
aptitudes I had always considered effortless, like an eye for
detail, were wholly contingent on my engagement and interest. "The minute that the Chinese college graduate leaves his
racial group to seek a position elsewhere marks his introduction into a world of professional rivalry, racial antagonism,
petty jealousy and social maneuvering," Grace Wang declared
in a 1936 speech to the New York–based Chinese Women's
Association. But had I ever been with my "racial group"? What
struggles, asks Jay Caspian Kang, did "those of us born in the
seventies and eighties" share with the Chinese whose meager
purchase on this continent ran from the Gold Rush to the
conscious coinage of identity in the 1968 Berkeley protests?
We were taught, the Korean American writer asserts, "that the
civil rights movement had fixed everything and all salvation
could be earned through equal competition in the academy
and then in the workforce." And so, as poet Cathy Park Hong
acridly demurs, "I must, without complaint, prove myself in
the workforce," a good son of Hart-Celler, a chip off the mono-
lith, the "ideal neoliberal subject." I measured my success in

the city, somewhat fancifully, by the number of windows I got to gaze out at it from, the higher or more private, the better—a privileged infiltration. Between the fact that I was now being paid to read—in French, no less!—and the location of the agency's offices, overlooking Union Square, I felt like I'd put one over on the world, a feat I'd always valued all the more for its feeling patriotic; the only true American life is having gotten away with it. This was an era of cover letters: selves summed up, pared down to a paragraph of accomplishments. I was submitting other people's fiction but also my own, under aliases that my girlfriend at the time thought all sounded like "porn names," claiming publication credits in nonexistent lit mags of my own invention. I'd heard that while working at the Academy of American Poets, Jeffrey Eugenides would type out a greeting on letterhead and, under this cover, devote the body of his correspondence to drafting *The Virgin Suicides*. What an asshole, I thought, as on weekends, alone at the mail machine on the fifteenth floor overlooking Union Square, I weighed and stamped my own stories, paperwork for unclaimed property to the State of New Jersey, and, eventually, translations by Edward Gauvin.

In November 2005, I received the news of my father's demise, the final step in an intermittent and protracted process of leave-taking that had begun when I was fifteen and my brother was six. Despite ever-longer absences from home, on trips to the various American cities where his latest job as a mainframe software engineer had taken him, he remained a presence in my life, manifesting mostly in erratic, contentious holiday visits during high school and irksome early morning phone calls at college, until giving up the ghost on a patch of land in China whose name I will never now know. My brother took the train down from New Haven, where he had just started at Yale, and together we raised a glass in a dark Chelsea bar to the man who had become Thomas when, in 1968, he immigrated from Taiwan to America for his second master's degree. "Do you know why he picked that name?" my brother asked. "I think he told me once it sounded honest," I said. "Honest Tom." We agreed that neither of us had ever heard that epithet before.

Any evidence I have that "Edward Gauvin" really helped me get published is entirely circumstantial. How could it be otherwise? The torturous, compulsory literary initiation known as submission is a black box. All I can say is this: The very first translation I sent out as Edward Gauvin was accepted. As were the next two, and, save for the two after that, the next five, always on the first try. "It never ceases to amaze me," writes Christopher L. Miller in his history of literary hoaxes, "how—when you're looking at a single sentence and sometimes even a single word—it can change back and forth before your eyes depending on who you think the author is." Call it luck; credit it to skill (in writing) or taste (in fiction), buying into the myth of American meritocracy, in which quality is always self-evident, its criteria unchanging, and their foundations never examined. With translation, I achieved a dream that had eluded my own fiction: that of letting my work speak for itself—paradoxically, by having it speak for others. It's not that being Edward Gauvin, with its Francophone echo, gave me an advantage; it's that *not* being Asian removed a handicap. When editors, after years of working correspondence, finally put a face to my name, that face surprises them. But the name forestalls the question that is like a job-interview variation on "No, but where are you really from?"—namely, "How did you come by your French?" Which only echoes the question I was often asked at Iowa, "Why don't you write about your parents?"

Yes, EDWARD GAUVIN is a graduate of the Iowa Writers' Workshop, a fact he often, and to others' incredulity, omits from his résumé. Well, why not? He wasn't yet Edward Gauvin there, and by the time he was, he wanted a fresh start. In becoming Edward, he'd asked no favors of Iowa; having left with few friends and impressed no teachers, whom would he have asked? A year in, he'd tried to flee, and that was how he'd wound up in the office of the program administrator, Connie Brothers, inquiring about the policy for a leave of absence. "We don't generally grant those," she said. "We like to get people in and out in two years. It's really not a very long time." To buck him up, she did something she was "not supposed to do," and after rummaging in a filing cabinet, returned with the letter of recommendation that had surely sealed his acceptance, from T. C. Boyle. "Dear Frank," it read, "don't let this one get away"—a single sentence on an otherwise-blank sheet of paper in that gawky, swooping, imperious scrawl with which he would autograph his books to me, never failing to misspell my name.

From what is now called Chongqing, ROBERT DUNN WU began penning a column for the stateside publication *Chinese News*, the successor to the defunct *Chinese Digest*. In his first piece, he writes, "The urge to set foot on Free China soil had kidnapped me. I could not resist." Chinese American author Amy Tan has said that when she first set foot in China, she "became Chinese." Australian photographer William Yang reports: "I've had the experience that the ex-patriot [*sic*] American writer Amy Tan describes... Although it didn't quite happen like that for me I know what Amy's talking about. The experience is very powerful and specific, it has to do with land, with standing on the soil of the ancestors and feeling the blood of China run through your veins." I never felt as Tan did, or Yang, but whether it was because I didn't plant my foot down firmly enough, or because the ground was insufficiently giving, who can say? During my year in Taipei, I felt, at the end of a long day, like I'd gone to Chinatown for groceries and now couldn't get home. In *Metropolitan*, Whit Stillman's apologia for the "urban haute bourgeoisie" (you couldn't find a WASPier film if you tried), the nebbishly bespectacled Charlie Black, played by Taylor Nichols, is asked if he's had the religious experience he describes and defends in such rhapsodic if unrehearsed detail. "Uh, no," he stammers. "I—I hope to someday."

By the time ISAMU NOGUCHI arrived at Arizona's Poston War Relocation Center, in May 1942, he had called upon a roster of such eminences as Clare Booth Luce, Archibald MacLeish, Carey McWilliams, Paul Robeson, and J. Robert Oppenheimer in his efforts to raise awareness of the plight of Japanese Americans. But it was John Collier, director of the Bureau of Indian Affairs, organizer of the Wheeler-Howard "Indian New Deal," and energetic reviver of indigenous American arts and crafts, who enabled Noguchi's voluntary internment at Poston, built on the Colorado River Indian Reservation over the objections of the Tribal Council. Disappointed by New York, where "not a single communist" or radical leftist friend spoke up against Roosevelt's Executive Order 9066, Noguchi showed up brimming with ambitions for teaching art and designing "an ideal cooperative community." He opened a wood carving and carpentry shop but was allowed no tools except those he had brought with him and was forced to scavenge materials from camp-building contractors and the surrounding desert. In his mind were plans for parks, baseball fields, swimming pools, a cemetery, even an irrigation system, but in his hands was clay that he spent rote days turning into bricks. The strictures of camp life only heightened the unforgiving harshness of the climate. The War Relocation Authority, to whom Noguchi was a nuisance, had no intention of more permanently settling this desert wilderness, much less of leaving behind evidence of these makeshift installations after the war. Noguchi's half sister, Ailes Gilmour, a dancer with the Martha Graham Dance Company, wrote from New York: "Can you really do so much staying there with them or are you punishing yourself?" By late July, the "haunting sense of unreality, of not quite belonging" that had made him "seek for an answer among the Nisei" had given way to severe despondency "for lack of companionship," Noguchi wrote to John Collier. Lacking the "same history," the "same background," Noguchi found "there was a lot of resentment" toward, at best, an outsider modeling values of integration and democracy, or, at worst, a "half-breed" agent of the administration. Biracial, overtly political, and, at thirty-seven, between the ages of the Nisei and their Issei parents, Noguchi reportedly donned "geta clogs that he had made himself" for the communal mess hall while sporting "high-heeled cowboy boots and a pith helmet" to collect mesquite wood from the desert. Twenty-five-year-old Henry Kanegae, who, like many of his generation, had been forced to drop out of college for lack of employment prospects, recalled that he "never saw [Noguchi] talking to any of the other internees" and that he always ate "quickly by himself, then went right back to his room"—a room the same size as the one Kanegae shared with his family. Seventy-six days after the sacrifice of his self-incarceration, Noguchi formally requested his release. His time at Poston, he said, had "knocked out my sense of social responsibility." But as Army Intelligence had tagged him as a "suspicious person" for his activities on behalf of Japanese Americans after Pearl Harbor, the request stalled in paperwork for one hundred and eight more days, at which point he was given a short-term furlough. "I have every expectation of coming back here in a month," he told the camp newsletter, the *Poston Bulletin*. "Until then I wish to say 'Sayonara for a while' to all my friends in Poston." Meanwhile, he wrote to his sister Ailes, "Please let my various friends know that I am on my way. I feel like Rip Van Winkle." At 9:00 p.m. on November 12, 1942, Noguchi was at the wheel of his Ford station wagon headed into the vast American night, never to return.

"I went too young" is what I usually say when people ask me why I had such a bad time at Iowa, because in the absence of memorably enumerable grievances, it's easier to loiter in inconclusion, ambiently blaming myself. Crowded into seminars and workshops during rounds of first-week intro-ductions, we told of the lives we'd left to come here. You could see how that gave the precocious a lot to live up to, or how a naïf might think he had the most to hide. We would, we were told, become a "community," though what people outside the workshop called it was a "hothouse." What Iowa taught me was that your past, or your lack thereof, could be leveraged against you as the limits of your imagination.

It wasn't so much charitable fact-checking as a refusal, on the basis of biography, to suspend disbelief. It was laughing behind your back, and something very literary, actually— reading your peers as characters, to be known more truly and completely than they knew themselves, their best needs and hidden desires. At Iowa, the land of writing what you know, it was clear to everyone but myself that what I knew best was being Asian American.

To point out that T. C. Boyle serially misspelled my name makes it sounds like it offended me. When you're born under the sign of belatedness, and your main relationship to the world is one of uncertainty, many things that might seem like they should offend lodge less in the craw than in the mind, where, as the years go by, they are endlessly turned over. I regarded the misspelling with a quizzical detachment that was not, to the best of my knowledge, a strategic psychological insulation from some truth I did not want to face. I found amusing the Rorschach nature of it all, a blot I would never get to the bottom of. Nothing would resolve the mystery short of direct questioning, an act as rarely dared in life as it is accepted in fiction, that great assuager of life's shortcomings, such that when fiction fails to supply this, we accuse it of playing coy for the sake of plot. It could've been an innocent oversight, left uncorrected and hardened into habit. Or, as I sometimes imagined, a discrepancy noticed at some point but persisted in as a "Boy Named Sue"–style provocation, to see if I would ever speak up. "I knew a husband and wife who still use *vous* with each other," once said the man I came to think of as my "French father," although he was British. He and his French wife both taught English, and loved, in the guise of an education, to regale me with explorations of linguistic quirks, the fodder of their connubial life. I had been wondering when, if at all, to broach the question of switching to *tu* with Châteaureynaud, whom, at the time of the conversation, I had known for three years. "Ah well, then it's too late!" my French father merrily exclaimed. To everything there is a season.

The epithet is, of course, HONEST JOHN (c. 1930–), as in Smith, Doe, or Q. Public, and not *Thomas*, as in Doubting (according to John). I don't think he was an apostle familiar to my father, who in his fifties—though I'd never really known him to believe in Jesus—went so far as to say Christ was only for white people—that is, in an afterlife to which he gave full credence, and in which the social constructs of this fallen world seemed to have been divinely reified, the Son of Man would not shepherd those Chinese foolish enough to have worshipped him. But whyever not? Wasn't this the land where, as Pat Buchanan wrote during Barack Obama's 2008 campaign, "600,000 black people, brought from Africa in slave ships, grew into a community of 40 million [and] were introduced to Christian salvation"? "I pity them," my father said, without interrupting the slow, measured motions of the qigong he had taken up, the only salve for his hypochondria now that he had lost all faith in Western medicine. A few years later, he would join Falun Gong, finally going where my mother refused to follow. It was by searching under the name Thomas that, at her urging, I reclaimed from the state of New Jersey a few shares my father had bought in various corporations, the dividends of desultory enthusiasms lost to successive address changes, totaling just over one thousand dollars, the sum of any fiscal inheritance I was ever to receive.

I did not attend an Ivy League institution. I did not, as my father advised when informed of my writerly aspirations, attend Harvard Law School and, after working as a corporate lawyer, eventually become a high-tech litigation consultant. My filial piety did not extend to studying medicine, improving my Mandarin, or doing time in a major firm as a software engineer. I did not "secure a firm foundation before pursuing artistic ambitions," because I did not believe in, or could not wait for, a someday of spare time in which I might write. Nor did I foresee that the kids who mocked the smell of the dumplings my mother packed me in a thermos for lunch would grow up, move to the city, and become fashionably conversant in dim sum. Instead, I scrimped and struggled through a string of odd jobs that left me no time to write, doing my best to ignore the popularity of the Chinese literature I did not translate, now hotly discussed over sushi and bulgogi, for whose screen adaptations I was not asked to consult or executive-produce.

Instead, I advocate for higher translators' wages in what scant free time remains now that I have a child, whom I strive to support in some approximation of the comfort my parents afforded me. As the parenting class my wife and I were attending drew to a close with our daughter's first Christmas, it occurred to me, in approaching the pyramid of gift bags with my own white elephant, that my main claim to the middle class was being able to lead a book group.

When GEORGES-OLIVIER CHÂTEAUREYNAUD was three years old, his father was deported to Nazi Germany for obligatory wartime labor, although he would continue to be a presence in his son's life, retaining, even long after the war had ended, his habit of turning up unannounced with effusive gifts, a younger woman, a harebrained scheme, a short temper. Critics have described Châteaureynaud's protagonists as lost children, soft-hearted and naive, unsuited to life's casual cruelties. In 2013, Châteaureynaud published, in the one-hundredth issue of *Brèves*, a review devoted to short fiction, his translation of H. V. Chao's story "My Father's Hand."

The titular character of Châteaureynaud's "LE COURTIER DELAUNAY" (1988) is a secretive antiques broker noted in the business for his uncanny ability to procure any item, answering in every last detail to a client's most exacting specifications. Small wonder, then, that he excites the curiosity and cupidity of the narrator, antiquarian Edmond Thyll, who despite firm warnings cannot resist the temptation to violate Delaunay's sole stipulation: that he never be asked where he gets his goods. Breaking into Delaunay's apartment, Thyll finds the broker's harrowing journal of the ordeals he suffers in trafficking objects of desire from another world into our own. The gift horse's orifice thus thoroughly surveyed, Delaunay breaks off his dealings with Thyll, who is left alone, comfortless, and unrequited, with the copy he has made of "the only diary of the fantastic in the history of literature."

EDWARD GAUVIN and I were friends for a few months, as is the fickle nature of first grade. I have a photo of myself at his birthday party from that time: pointy hats and red-eye in that jaundiced blur of 110 Kodak film snapped on a cheap Instamatic, with its upright flashbulbs like a miniature tray of ice cubes. I recall G.I. Joes that I coveted, carelessly strewn on artificial rocks edging his backyard pool—the very sort of stagy, rugged setting where I never dared sully my own action figures but always saw in commercials during the half-hour cartoons I'd quickly switch off whenever I heard the garage door rumbling open. It was a short, steep drive from our house to Edward's, in a leafy enclave of older money, among houses of classmates whose parents were dentists or otolar-yngologists, though I associated it mostly with my piano teacher. During the Revolutionary War, the Continental Army had camped nearby, looking out over the plains toward

New Brunswick, a fact commemorated every July 4 with a changing of the flag and a reading of the Declaration of Independence. This was on the "east" side of town, which despite belonging to the same district as the "west," had its own set of schools; east-siders would go on to a middle school named Hillside, its soccer fields and basketball courts built into the slope. We lived on Foothill Road. You can't make up these names, their on-the-nose class topography. That spring, I tested into a gifted-and-talented program, where I spent the next four years beloved for my intelligence and imagination. After fifth grade, my family moved to the west side of town, starting me in middle school not at Hillside but Eisenhower, where I was despised and ostracized for my intelligence and imagination. In my thirties, I realized a large part of my life had been devoted to engineering, then eschewing, environments where I could be thought of as intelligent, which was the only way I could imagine being loved. I wanted people who loved me to admire me, and I thought people who admired me loved me.

In T. C. Boyle's office—with that photo on the wall of him posed as Springsteen from the cover of *Born to Run*—I felt smart, an undergrad freshly returned from a semester abroad in Edinburgh with *The Granta Book of the American Short Story* edited by Richard Ford in one hand, querying him about every name in its table of contents, begging explications of specific lines from Donald Barthelme's "The Indian Uprising" (you see, there *was* direct questioning). "You, my friend, have to go to Iowa," he told me. "You belong there." More than a decade later, Edward Gauvin sat in T. C. Boyle's office with something like a feeling of defeat and gratitude. Defeat, because here he was again, after all these years, *considering going back to grad school*, a euphemism for a certain kind of spiritual despair. And gratitude, because he hadn't realized how much he missed someone who complimented his writing and cared about whether he kept it up. He wanted to apologize for not having made good on his apparent promise at Iowa, but he also wanted to ask, Why me? Why there? "When they were reviewing applications, Frank Conroy called me up to ask about you," Boyle offered. "He said, 'You know, this story is all... made up.' I told him, 'Frank, why does that matter?'"

Into every life the unaccountable must come, and the FANTASTIQUE (c. 1830–) is on hand to reify it into irreducible monstrosity. Classically, the subgenre, born of German Romanticism and flowering evilly in France's belle epoque, revolves around an inexplicable, seemingly impossible phenomenon briefly visited upon the protagonist—what critic and Surrealist Roger Caillois called "a rift, or tear... an almost unbearable irruption." "The crack in the teacup opens / A lane to the land of the dead," a crooked path readers raised on realism rush to understand as metaphor, that passport to literary class-climbing, extrapolated from scraps of alleged psychology. But this the true fantastic refuses, its enigma supremely intact: "eine sich ereignete unerhörte Begebenheit." This meeting, never mortal, is the pivot of a life forever altered. There is now a before and an after; the encounter has made you a survivor, seared by witness borne and still burning with the desire to be welcomed back into humanity's fold with what now lies beyond reach: others' credence and acceptance. How many of us, freshly returned from a foreign land, find it hard to interest others in an account of our time there? How often, over the breakfast table or a lover's pillow, has a bewitching dream frayed to tatters in the retelling? How do we negotiate our return from the unrepeatable and unprovable; how to import solitary experience into a world of consensual meaning? Isn't this the very loneliness from which literature vows to save us? "It is certain my conviction gains infinitely," wrote Novalis, "the moment another soul will believe in it." In sociologist and historian Tzvetan Todorov's famous formulation, the crucial feature of the fantastic as a mode is the choice it leaves readers: between realism and fabulism, natural and supernatural, madness and marvel—though as New Weird novelist Michael Cisco points out, it can be both. (Only a Cartesian would find them mutually exclusive.) The act of immigrating, Salman Rushdie once remarked, is like a self-inflicted mental illness.

I claim never to have asked Iowa for anything in establishing myself as a translator, but that isn't entirely true. A Fulbright application required institutional affiliation, and so, after more than a decade, Edward Gauvin returned to Iowa City for the first time, to hear a committee of professors and administrators review his materials. Let no one say he had no friends: in the midst of a divorce and down with a cold, the friend he stayed with slept on the sofa anyway, giving Gauvin the single bed in the chilly room he was renting, down a dismal hall from a shared microwave and sink. Gauvin could not resist walking by the Dey House, nor, once he was there, ducking in. There it stood, atop a relative promontory of rock and memory overlooking the Iowa River; the donations that had since given it a modern annex held no candle to his own mythologizing tendencies, which had added a mansard-roofed tower, or rather, superimposed, over that modest Victorian residence, Edward Hopper's *House by the Railroad*. Names come and go—the workshop accepts fifty students each year—but Deb and Jan in the front office, and Connie in her own just behind, all knew my face. Connie warmly ushered me over to see the only professor who happened to be on hand—one whose workshop I had, from fear, malaise, or anomie, stopped attending in my last semester there, as if daring him to somehow impede my imminent graduation (the result: a B-minus). We'd never really spoken at length, and now seemed equally at a loss for conversation. "I'm writing a MacArthur recommendation for Yiyun Li," he said. "Do you two know each other?" This teacher, who had always liberally lent out books to students, now offered me a can of Coke from his office mini-fridge, and I, recalling a rumor that the college was bound by contract to replace any books students neglected to return, wondered if there wasn't a rider in there, too, about keeping the minifridge stocked.

Born and raised in Somerville, New Jersey, poet EDWARD GAUVIN (1976–) earned his bachelor's degree from the University of Southern California and his MFA from the University of Iowa. He has been a Pushcart Prize nominee, cowinner of the Manchester Poetry Prize, and a finalist for the Brittingham and Felix Pollak Prizes in Poetry as well as the May Swenson Poetry Award. His poems have appeared in *Poetry*, the *Georgia Review*, the *Iowa Review*, *New Letters*, *Washington Square Review*, *Fugue*, the *Greensboro Review*, the *North American Review*, and the *Baltimore Review*. In 2015, having had a poem rejected forty times under his own name, Gauvin resubmitted it under the nom de plume of a Chinese American high school classmate, after which it was published in the University of Nebraska's literary journal *Prairie Schooner*, and went on to be selected for that year's edition of *The Best American Poetry* series. Am I an Asian American dreaming that I'm a white man, or a white man dreaming that I'm an Asian American?

The posthumously published *Memoirs of* **** (1764) revealed that Formosa was not the first island nation of which GEORGE PSALMANAZAR had tried to pass himself off as a native. En route to Germany at the age of sixteen to see his father for the first time in a decade, he obtained, for his claims of being an Irish pilgrim headed to Rome, documents enabling him to journey in greater comfort on embezzled charity. Betrayed by a lack of knowledge of Ireland's language and landscape, he next set his sights on Japan, compensating for his equal ignorance of Japanese by inventing for it a twenty-six-character alphabet. Although his *Historical and Geographical Description of Formosa*, startling in its resemblance to early science fiction, eventually made his reputation, he was, having shortsightedly sold the rights for a pittance, to prove impecunious in his old age, when society had begun to doubt his authenticity. He was reduced to penning entries for encyclopedias and making public displays of ingesting tobacco or laudanum in quantities that would have felled a lesser addict. But in their avowed influence on Jean-Jacques Rousseau, and thus credibly on the modern genre as we know it—secular, literary, confessional—what may have secured Psalmanazar a more lasting posterity were his *Memoirs*, in which he never once revealed the name he was given at birth.

There were several Asian Americans in the Black Panther Party, but lifelong civil rights activist RICHARD MASATO AOKI (1938–2009) was the only one to be a founding member and, as field marshal, to hold a formal leadership position. A third-generation Japanese American, he was torn from his native California at age four and interned with his family at Utah's Topaz Relocation Center, from which he returned to an Oakland transformed by the influx of African Americans come to work in the wartime defense industry. Soon, with a paper route supplemented by shoplifting and "midnight auto supply" runs to rob junkyards, Aoki boasted of being "the toughest Oriental out of West Oakland," someone who stopped a gang fight with a "spelling bee on the street." When a truant officer caught up with him and his younger brother, David, they were sent to live with their now-divorced mother, who supported them as a laundress. At Herbert Hoover Junior High, Aoki scored in the genius range on the Stanford-Binet IQ Test and graduated as co-valedictorian. His dreams full of decorated veterans Audie Murphy and Ben Kuroki, he enlisted in hopes of becoming a pilot, a "warrior," and "a man by the standards of the 'Hood," if not "the first Japanese American general." After eight years—as a sharpshooter, medic, X-ray technician, and reservist— Aoki grew disillusioned with the war in Vietnam and this, together with his political awakening as a laborer, led him to leave the military and enroll at Merritt Community College in Oakland, where he befriended Huey P. Newton and Bobby Seale. Aoki trained the Panthers to use firearms from his personal collection, joining them on "shotgun patrols," during which they tailed police with cameras and tape recorders. Shortly after transferring to UC Berkeley in 1966, Aoki was elected to the Berkeley Young Socialist Alliance's executive council. He was also active in the Socialist Workers Party, the anti-war Vietnam Day Committee, and the Asian American Political Alliance. In the winter of 1969, he was a leading figure in the strike for the Third World College, which resulted in the founding of Berkeley's Department of Ethnic Studies, where Aoki, upon completing his master's degree, was among the first to teach. "I've seen where unity amongst the races yielded positives results," said Aoki. "I don't see any other way for people to gain freedom, justice, equality here except by being inclusionist." Over the next twenty-five years, he worked as a counselor, instructor, and administrator in the Peralta Community College District, before retiring in 1994. According to friends, colleagues, and relatives, Aoki had a way of staying connected to people; he was able, close friend Shoshana Arai told a reporter, to maintain friendships even during times when groups disagreed or became fractioned. Arai said: "Richard is probably one of the most amazingly loyal people I've ever met in my life." Like a well-meaning parent, he would send friends newspaper clippings; if there was a book he liked, he would buy multiple copies and give them away. Thirty years after spearheading the original strike, Aoki returned to campus to support student demonstrators when budget cuts endangered the Department of Ethnic Studies. In March 2009, an email made the rounds ascribing his demise "to complications from longstanding medical problems." Or, as a close friend once put it: "Richard... You got diabetes. You got hypertension. You got heart problems. You Black." Over five hundred people attended a four-hour service featuring martial arts, musical performances, and a eulogy from Yuri Kochiyama at UC Berkeley's Wheeler auditorium, whose burning had marked the beginning of the Third World strike four decades earlier. UC Santa Barbara professor Diane C. Fujino saluted him in her biography as a *Samurai Among Panthers*, and Seale remembered Aoki fondly as "one consistent, principled person who stood up and understood the international necessity for human and community unity in opposition to oppressors and exploiters." A year later, the Richard Aoki Memorial Committee revealed in a public statement that his death was due to a "bullet wound of the abdomen," as reported by the coroner, who had ruled it a suicide. He had no wife or children. In 2012, reporter Seth Rosenfeld obtained, through a Freedom of Information Act request, FBI records suggesting that Richard Aoki, widely esteemed as a "militant who had succeeded within the establishment without surrending [*sic*] to it," had in fact been a government informant from 1961 to 1977. These allegations were greeted with outrage and disbelief by an admiring and devoted community, some suggesting that they were an attempt to place a "snitch jacket" on a revered and beloved figure. Reader, do you know how I greeted this late-breaking twist? I felt... seen.

I don't know that I have, as the interview usually goes, wanted to be a writer ever since I was a child, or if ending up as a writer was merely the most common excuse I encountered, usually below the author's photo on the back flaps of library-jacketed books, for having had a series of odd jobs.

These were jobs, I presumed, that one walked into, never imagining they might take time and effort, much less experience, education, or connections, to secure. I pictured them more as unloading crates from a truck behind a supermarket, making a brief difference in a stranger's life, and moving on—*Sayonara for a while*—like Dr. Richard Kimble or Bill Bixby's Bruce Banner, hounded by regret but also lured by hope, keeping my head low in a big country where no one knew my name. In the land where anyone could be anything, I would try everything, and in so doing, in claiming the motley lives I was entitled to by birth, I'd enact something quintessentially American—I, the stereotype become archetype. Later, as being a writer began to seem likelier, or at least the best recoupment of years literally spent, there were other books with other kinds of capsule biographies, listing grants, degrees, visiting positions. I think I conceived a longing, then, to be a Guggenheim Fellow the same way I'd wanted to be a roustabout. But even had I realized this at the time, I wouldn't have allowed myself to know it. My wife, herself a writer, once remarked that while most people seem to build a story from the ground up, like a house, first laying the foundations and lastly concerning themselves with the trim, I seemed to pick a mood, a color, and then build, from the outside in, the semblance of a house using only paint chips. I approached life itself, you might say, like a British actor—a tic, a bit of putty, a résumé credit, a stage name. I thought the way to being an author was to have an "About the Author" page like everyone else's, but that only made sense, because what I really wanted to be was everyone else. "What makes all autobiographies worthless, is, after all, their mendacity," Freud wrote his nephew in a letter refusing an American offer to publish his memoirs. My high school classmate's name wasn't Edward Gauvin. Give me some credit. Names have been changed to protect the innocent.

In his essay "When Fiction Lives in Fiction," a rumination on the mise en abyme, Jorge Luis Borges, in Esther Allen's translation, attributes to Arthur Schopenhauer these words: "dreaming and wakefulness are the pages of a single book… to read them in order is to live, and to leaf through them at random, to dream." In the early months of 2021, I settled into the closest I've ever come, in my adult life, to a regular car commute. The year before had seen four moves, but home these days is wherever my wife and daughter are. In a series of short-term rentals, we orbited my aging, lung-damaged mother, come to rest in a bungalow in a gated Sacramento retirement community. Every other day, I would drive my toddler to what childcare looked like for us during the high pandemic: mornings with her grandmother, and then, as she outgrew naps, afternoons too. As I crossed the withered Yolo Basin wetlands, the interstate stretching before me seemed in a familiar American mirage to promise that this newfound routine, the reprieve of its relative certainty, would extend, if not forever, then at least indefinitely. And it did—for almost two years that, just two weeks after they came to an end, felt like forever ago. Early childhood and slow-burn crises share such bounded eternities, punctuated equilibriums. Months unmindful of rain or shine, and then the Sierras rising snow-capped from the clouds, like a friend whose hair has suddenly gone white. Note to self: buy my osteoporotic mother a subscription to a medical alert service. Egrets painstakingly high-stepping through a field in whose deepening green the spring's new rapeseed blossoms gleamed like night's first stars. On the radio, a San Francisco woman was being interviewed about buying her elderly mother a Taser. The final leg of the drive ran down a crumbling isthmus of asphalt flanked by irrigation ditches, a favorite of herons and turtles, between phone lines low-slung from poles or coiled at splice cases like a lasso at a cowboy's hip. "Today marks the fortieth anniversary of Vincent Chin's murder." Glare from irrigation ponds between the causeway pilings, diamonds among splinters.

One August afternoon, I pulled into my mother's driveway beneath a dark orange sky. A grass fire had broken out not five miles away, at the airport, and I stepped from the car to a sight I had never before seen: ashes, dawdling dreamily down through the acrid beige air. My eyes burned. My first thought was: But it looks nothing like snow.

HEATH LEDGER

by OLIVIA GALLO

Translated from the Spanish by KIT MAUDE

CLOWNS WERE EVERYWHERE THAT summer. They wandered the outskirts of the city along semi-deserted roads, in quiet suburbs, and, at night, in the plazas. But you never actually met anybody who'd seen one in person—it was always someone like a cousin, or a friend of a friend. The rest of us had to make do with videos of sightings on the news and in social media compilations. For instance, one was filmed from a car parked by the side of a road at night. A clown approached in the dark, spotlighted in the yellow headlights. They were always knock-offs of the Joker, these anti-clowns. Heath Ledger's messed-up version, not the Jack Nicholson one: wild green hair, makeup smudged like it had been rubbed with a wet cloth. There were variations in the outfit, though. The clown in the car video was wearing red overalls with big white polka dots and yellow Dr. Martens. He crept toward the car. The guy filming wasn't much older than a teenager, and his voice sounded like it had only recently broken. There were more guys around his age in the car, asking questions, laughing, and lapsing into stunned silence, all at the same time, a chorus. When the clown got very close, the driver started to back up. Then there were screams as the clown broke into a run.

Gonzalo and I moved into his grandmother's house in Belgrano R that same summer. It was dirty and empty. We dropped the mattress in the living room because Gonzalo didn't want to move the TV into the main bedroom, where his grandmother had slept. We spent the rest of the inheritance on alcohol, pot, and Chinese food, all of which we consumed in bed, half-naked between synthetic sheets.

I don't know whether I really was happy, but I thought I was, for a time. I'd just finished college and that summer I left the house in Belgrano R only for obligatory dinners with my parents, to which Gonzalo did not accompany me in spite of his offers, from bed, just as I was leaving the house.

"You want me to come with?"

He knew the answer was no.

My parents were worried about me, but they didn't say so outright. When I was looking the other way, my mother would try to fill my plate with a second helping. My father would ask me how things were going in an unconvincingly casual tone.

My friends complained over WhatsApp that they never saw me. They were annoyed at first, then worried. Then they just stopped including me in their plans. For the first time in my life, I didn't mind being left out.

Gonzalo and I had a fairly fixed routine: We'd wake up at around two in the afternoon; he'd shower first, then me, and sometimes we'd go together. Our breakfast consisted of soggy expired cereal with maté. We'd watch TV, go out to buy cigarettes and something for lunch (generally pasta), and eat it watching TV. Then we'd fuck and fall asleep. Once we'd woken up, Gonzalo would go out to buy vodka or beer, we'd eat the leftovers from lunch or order takeout, drink, and smoke pot when we had it. Then we'd watch more TV, fuck again, and pass out at about three or four in the morning.

Gonzalo woke up several times a night. In his nightmares, he'd kick the air without realizing it. The sheets, which were already damp, would get damper. At some point, he'd sit up and curl into a ball with his head between his knees. He'd sit like that for a while, like he'd just gotten some bad news. I'd rub his slick back or get him a glass of water. Then he'd go back to sleep for a while, sometimes clinging to my waist, sometimes with his back to me.

The only other person allowed to enter the house in Belgrano R was Mateo. He'd been a close friend of Gonzalo's brother in high school and was the first to find the body after he jumped from the balcony. He had been in the apartment Gonzalo and his brother had shared on the seventeenth floor. Gonzalo wasn't there so his brother had asked Mateo to buy his medication. The pharmacy was a block away.

Sometimes I imagine Mateo coming back from the pharmacy, one hand in his jeans pocket and the other carrying a bag full of pills, walking toward the corner of República de la India and Seguí. The body fell on the Seguí side, so Mateo wouldn't have seen it if he'd taken República de la India. I think about the name of the street, *Seguí*, "keep going," picturing it as a neon warning sign: NOT THIS WAY. KEEP GOING. Beforehand, would he have seen the horrified expression of the janitor in the building opposite, or blood splattered on the curb? Would he have had an inkling of what had happened before he saw his dead friend with his own eyes?

I could barely remember how Gonzalo's brother looked, even though I'd met him on three or four occasions. The first time was in my junior year of high school, on my first visit to their house. The apartment on República de la India and Seguí was a duplex, and the bedrooms were upstairs, separated by a bathroom. When I left Gonzalo's bedroom to pee, I heard someone say, "Psst." Gonzalo's brother's door was half-open and I could see him sitting at the computer, his face lit by the robotic blue glow of the screen, with the soundtrack to a video game playing in the background. He was smiling and waving at me to come over. I opened the door a little more and went halfway in, trying to hide my blue school uniform skirt. He asked me what my name was. I told him. His smile grew broader.

When Mateo and Gonzalo were together, they seemed to compete to see who could behave worse. Who spoke less, who sighed the most, who stared into space the longest. Whenever

I visited Gonzalo, generally at dinnertime, I offered to cook just to get away from the two of them.

The last time Mateo came to the house in Belgrano R, I was in the kitchen. I heard him talking about the clowns, telling Gonzalo that a friend of his had seen one as he was leaving a club, on the train tracks at the level crossing between Sucre and Montañeses. I heard Mateo say, "They're crazy, those guys. The barrier was down, according to my friend. And the clown was just standing there on the tracks. He didn't move." Gonzalo said something I didn't hear, to which Mateo answered that most people thought it was part of a publicity campaign for an upcoming horror movie featuring clowns, but he thought they were just guys who had nothing better to do. When I came out of the kitchen, Gonzalo asked what his friend had done. Mateo lit a cigarette before answering. Then he said, "The same thing as everyone else. He ran away."

After dinner, I sat alone with Mateo in the living room while Gonzalo did the dishes.

"You can't spend your lives locked up in here. It's not good for him or you."

I answered with a vague gesture, a kind of half smile accompanied by an eye roll, like I was saying, *What do you want me to do about it?* He finished his cigarette, stubbed it out in the glass ash tray, and leaned forward.

"I mean it. You need to get out."

I asked him where we would go. It sounded like a stupid question, but from the way he leaned back, I knew that Mateo

understood what I meant. We didn't think there was anywhere worth leaving the house for, Gonzalo especially. Mateo
took a brown leather wallet from his pants, from which he
removed a pair of tickets printed with multicolored man-
dalas. He put them down on the wooden table between us.

"Take these, and persuade him to go. Remind him how
much he used to enjoy these parties. It'll be good. I'm going.
I'll take you in my car."

I was dancing when Gonzalo put a hand on my shoulder.
I turned around. He didn't say a word. I asked him if he
wanted to leave. He nodded.

The sun was out. It was high summer, when dawn comes
early. It couldn't have been later than five. Gonzalo walked a
few steps ahead of me, and the sun beat down on his leather
jacket, making him gleam like a lizard. I asked if we should
take a taxi. Without looking back, he said that Mateo had
lent us the car. He took the keys from his pocket and held
them out. I hadn't remembered him being such a fast driver.
We turned onto Libertador, swerving past cars left and right.
I asked him to slow down. He looked at me and ran his
tongue over his teeth with his mouth closed, something he
did when he was annoyed. I asked him what was wrong.
"Nothing," he said, continuing to zigzag up Libertador until
he almost ran into a car stopped at a traffic light. The tires
screeched as he braked. The seat belt saved me from smash-
ing my forehead on the dashboard. Gonzalo didn't seem to
notice; he just went on driving like nothing had happened.
We went on a couple more blocks; I was staring at him,

waiting for him to do something, to apologize. When we got to the Argentine Car Association building, I told him I was getting out. He asked me why, but he didn't raise his voice at the end like he was asking a question. I undid the seat belt without answering. He took his hands off the wheel and held up his palms before stopping at a corner.

"Whatever."

I got out, slamming the door behind me.

I didn't want to go back to the house in Belgrano R, or to see my parents, so I went into the car association café. I ordered a coffee and sat by the window and there he was, in a violet outfit with blue stars, with that crooked, smudged smile, sitting a few tables away, reading a newspaper.

GET! GET! GET!

by VÉRONIQUE DARWIN

THE WORKERS ARE HIRED to do everything to our house so Mom and Dad don't have to get together. Mom says "get together" with a sexy hip swing. Dad calls it "negotiate."

One of the workers is the doughnut guy: he carries a toolbox, but it's made of paper and it's full of doughnuts. He cuts holes in walls and looks in with an eye squeezed shut, then calls people over to see if they see what he sees. They usually see the same thing, and tell him to do something about it. Instead he hoists his pants up, takes a bite from a doughnut, and does another hole.

At Christmas we make doughnuts of our own in vats of oil. Our French Canadian mother drinks hot wine, my dad disappears, I roll the dough, and my sister drops them in. Except she refuses to cook the hole balls. She always makes me roll more and more rings even though my tears make the dough too wet. Our bickering makes Mom laugh. Mom loves to laugh until she pees. I know my sister isn't yelling at me to be funny, or mean. She just didn't know until now that you can make doughnuts with just the holes.

Another worker we like is the painter. He wears thick white overalls with crusty colors that crinkle when he stands up from his coffee break. His big black beard is very colorful. When he rolls the paint on, he takes a deep breath, and when he lays it off, he sighs. He's painting but it sounds like he's sleeping.

My sister has the biggest crush on the transformer. We call him that because he has so many tools, it's like he's wearing different trucks as outfits. He even makes drill bits with his lips when he pees against the glass stucco on the side of the house. The other day my sister bent her head a certain way while peering out the attic window and told me she could see his penis. I told her I'm not interested in penises. I told her I'm ten. She said she is fifteen and she is deeply interested in them. I laughed like Mom when she said this.

I am a worker too. I am the youngest person ever to make the best coffee. I grind the beans fresh: I put them in a plastic bag and step on them on the concrete steps, or beat them against the stone fireplace. I boil the water to exactly one hundred degrees Celsius on the thermometer we use when we're sick. Whenever Dad comes to check on things, he announces that the only reason the work is going so well is because of my excellent coffee.

"He has no respect for the workers," says Mom. Last week she shouted that he didn't get it: the work was slow, but it was getting done. She uses the same verb for everything. She tells me to "get her glasses," or "get lost," or "get out," or "get with it." Sometimes she just shouts, "Get! Get! Get!" when I'm about to knock something over. I think that the verb *get* must be pretty powerful in her language, since it seems to stand in for any desire she has in the English-speaking world that Dad and my sister and I are a part of.

My sister works hard too. She has small assignments she makes for herself, even though it's summer. She copies out country-crossover song lyrics, makes MASH games for me even though it's supposed to be *my* ideas of *my* life, and phones friends and talks to them even when they don't pick up. She seems happier when she talks to herself, because then she can give and take the questions and answers she needs.

Dad and Mom sometimes put on beautiful billowing work shirts and join the workers, to make sure the details are just right. Dad is mostly interested in "resale value," while Mom keeps wanting to squeeze out her "dream home." Sometimes when they tape up paint swatches or walk on samples of wood flooring, they bump each other with their hips, or push each other with their hands. They are checking that the other is still there. What would they do if they were alone, or together?

When I was little, they were together and they were awful. When I was a bit older, they were alone and miserable. In the past couple years, they've been in between. The house keeps them that way: one upstairs, one down. My sister and I are the glue—the doughnut filling. We live on the main floor, with the TV and the front door and the kitchen. This is why I learned to make coffee. It's kind of a peace offering. It gets everyone to work.

I think I know how the house will turn out. It will be so perfect that we won't even want to live in it anymore. All of us will leave for different places. Mom will go to India with that yoga guy, Dad to the caves in France where he once lost his camera, my sister to medical school (one that doesn't use the MCATs, because she can't do standardized), and me to the factory. I want to learn to repeat and replicate. I want to watch coffee beans jiggling in their funnel, or doughnuts gliding by on their runway. I want to see the same thing over and over again. That's the kind of work that suits me.

One day we'll come back and find another family living here. They will be like us, only they'll have got all they needed. They won't even notice the house; they'll be too busy living in it.

MARTYRS

drawings by MORTEZA KHAKSHOOR

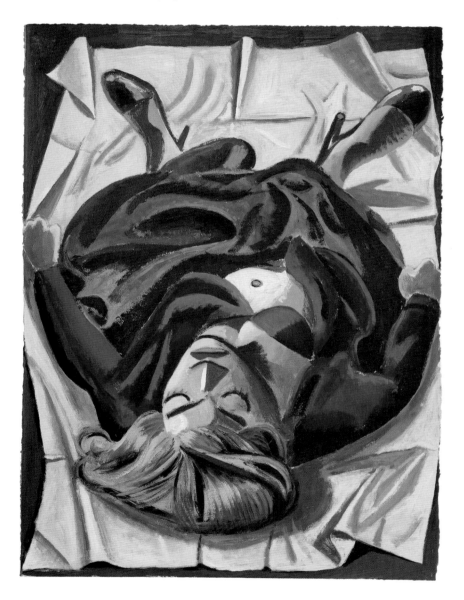

Blonded Martyr in Black Skirt

Martyrs is an ongoing series of drawings I began in late 2021, in response to the killing, in November 2019, of an unprecedented number of protesters in Iran—also known as Bloody November. This was by no means the first time the Iranian state had brutalized large numbers of civilian protesters. But the tragedy was greater this time, and I found myself unable to forget, ignore, or escape it.

This series is a personal lamentation, an homage to the suffering, the dispossessed, the defeated, and the murdered. These martyrs might be anywhere: on the streets of Iran, in a prison cell, in a morgue basement, or, indeed, anyplace in the world. They might be dead, unconscious, or merely asleep, but all are connected to those who have died, recently and throughout history, because of their opposition, resistance, and astonishing resolve.

—Morteza Khakshoor

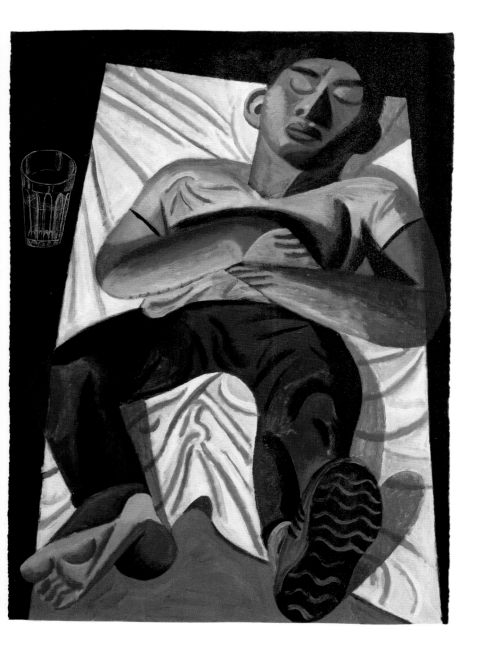

Martyr No. 3

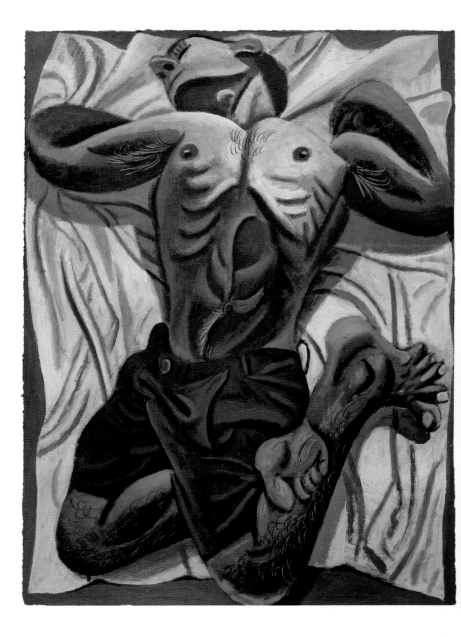

Small Martyr No. 4

Martyr No. 2

Small Martyr No. 2

Small Martyr No. 1

Martyr No. 6

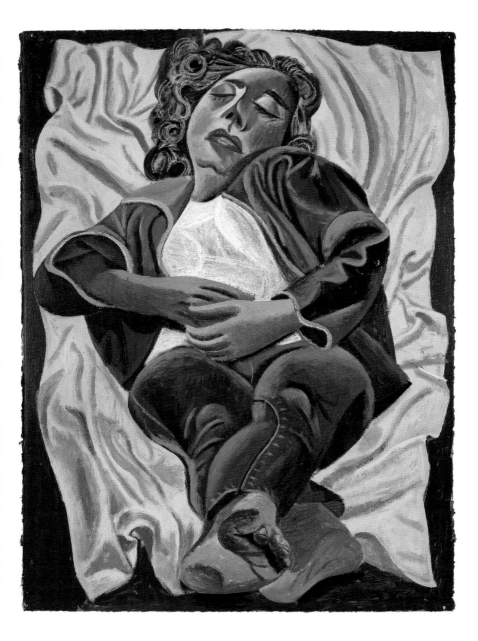

Blue-Jacketed Martyr

Martyr No. 12

Martyr No. 2

Martyr No. 10

Small Martyr No. 3

Martyr No. 5

Martyr No. 4

Martyr No. 7

THE SCIENCE FICTION WRITER

by EUGENE LIM

WHAT DID JANE KIM mean to me? Sometimes I wonder if she wasn't the main obelisk over my life—under whose shadow I ceaselessly toiled. Or was she a gruff cartoon, dropping notes of wisdom and then shoving me out of the nest, whispering fiercely even as I fell: *Fly or die!* I wanted her to be a friend, trading pro tips and triangulating our pinpoint coordinates, which were (it felt) forever dotting a fogged and dark and wild plain—but this scenario was less than unlikely. To Jane, I might have been a brief echo or a moment's charm, never enough weight to ever be significant, to be a threat. Or, even more likely, I was to her a housefly, waved at in annoyance or, in a moment of wild eruption, quickly murdered and forgotten.

I wanted her approval.

Though I wasn't one, I wanted her approval the way an orphan does—a mewling thing desperate for imprinting after self-transporting into a new tribe of titans.

My own parents were brilliant but unread strivers, immigrants whom I loved but whose sacrifices I could barely comprehend, let alone acknowledge or, the great dream: *pay back*. But something fateful had refashioned my second-gen status. I had secretly committed to an ambition. It was a decision like that, something spoken to oneself but at a volume just above cognition, liminal, in the background. I was fighting, a lifelong fight, for indulgence and liberation, even against their wishes, because my indulgent idleness and freedom from expectations were the veiled ambition of their sacrifices—a goal almost necessarily (but tragically) hidden from them. At least that was how I continuously, in those years, justified myself to myself. My parents' impoverishment and self-enslavement were intended to purchase *my* freedom, I had thought, repeatedly and regularly, with a complex shame and in an act of lifelong, slow-motion entrapment.

About five years had passed since I'd made a fool of myself on an obscure literary panel with Jane Kim. Even as I hoped she'd forgotten my gaffes, nonetheless I also hoped she remembered me. In the interim, Jane had published two extraordinary novels—books that seemed to capture her philosophy in a mastered form. As her reputation grew, as her rediscovery began, to her loyal fans—to me—she was the great open secret of

American letters, hidden in plain sight within the ghetto walls of genre, of science fiction, of the dismissed comic book team that Kemp had named : the What-If Bureau of Investigations.

I, too, had something to show for the intervening years. I had managed to eke out a draft of a novel—a slim and science-fictionally cloaked autofiction, wherein the heroine's quarry, which is none other than a disguised version of herself, constantly eludes, as chase is given through different worlds. Its tentative title was "Space Bar." At that point, the manuscript was clumsy and raw and taped together and full of unproven bravado. Of course, I thought it the next step in my ascension to the throne (of what?) and was airily convinced of its genius.

My plan was simple. I was going to knock on Jane Kim's front door and hand her the manuscript.

Here I am—can you see it?—in front of the inconspicuous townhouse with a bright maroon door on the outskirts of Philadelphia. I'd taken a long, cheap bus ride from New York and a short, expensive cab ride from the city center. In my hands I hold a manilla folder, thickened by the manuscript I'd freshly printed out that morning (and pored worryingly over the whole long bus trip).

Jane doesn't open the door. Instead, I find myself staring at a young woman in a crisp and generic outfit. Her clothes are so oddly formal that I assume—wrongly, it turns out—that she is Jane's nurse. I manage to blurt, "Is Jane Kim at home?"

"Who is it, Flora?" I recognize Jane's voice calling from the interior—clear, strong, fundamentally polite—and hear her steps approaching. A blush warms my cheeks as I feel my nerves starting to fail. Jane joins Flora at the door. I face them, a step below, feeling my puffed-up courage leaking like a fearful piss pooling at my feet. I practically whisper, "Hi, Jane."

She looks at me and focuses. I can see her mind whirl, her facial-recognition routines spinning in place, and then Jane says a sentence that hovers between question and statement: "You're a writer."

"Yes," I say quickly, adding, "we met a few years ago on a panel in New York. At the library. On virtual reality."

"Ah, yes." She smiles. "I remember." A long second. "Yes, well, come in, come in."

I softly exhale and enter.

Jane guides me into a crowded room that is charmingly (to me) sloppy: a desk with a large computer monitor under gradual siege by towers of papers and books—many familiar titles, many others intriguingly not; several steel utility shelves crammed with books and knickknacks (I think I spot a Nebula trophy on its side, being used as a bookend); three architect lamps in different muted hues clamped in strategic places (which Flora turns on during the subsequent magic hour); striking and surprising art on the walls (a beautiful black-and-gold abstraction captioned *the mind shaped by many fleeting emotions*, a watercolor of what looks like some kind of octopus, a framed front page of the Parisian newspaper *L'Express* from May 1968, a woodcut of an elderly couple struggling in the wind). Jane moves a stack of papers off the couch and gestures for me to sit in the now-open space while she takes a chair opposite. "Something to drink?" she offers, glancing at her watch. "I'm going to have a gin something."

"Um, yes. Please. The same."

"Flora, would you mind?" Flora nods that she doesn't and goes to prepare the drinks. Turning to me, Jane says, "Remind me your name? My memory isn't what it used to be."

I tell her, "Gene," and she smiles again.

"Oh yes. Youngblood." I manage to smile a bit, too, as if the nickname was something we'd come up with together, something palsy-walsy.

"That's right. That's what you called me."

Flora brings us the drinks. A sip seems to loosen us up. "Tell me about yourself, Youngblood."

The both superficial and fundamental quality I have in common with Jane—a writer who has used genre to embed an ongoing discussion on the state of Asian America—despite wide gulfs in personal histories and origin stories, is our so-called race. And yet even though I instantly feel this is the underlying bridge between us, I know also that bringing it up too immediately would attenuate it, will cheapen it. (In fact, our initial avoidance of mentioning it is, at the time, perhaps our most telling Korean American quality.)

"I've published a handful of stories. One in ————," and I name a prestige publication whose corporate aesthetic is to reassure that it is transcending its corporate aesthetic.

"Impressive," Jane says, almost convincingly.

On the tip of my tongue is a question I have heard Jane answer before, in formal interviews, where she had diluted her answer or deflected the question, which is admittedly an absurd one but the response to which I suspect is not. I want to ask her, *Do you think of yourself as a writer of science fiction?*, but instead I say, "And I've been working on a novel."

"That was going to be my next question," Jane says, smiling. She has on a T-shirt that I hadn't been able to read, due to a combination of nerves and its small font, but now that we are seated I see that it says, in tiny white letters on a black background, FUCK YOU YOU FUCKETY FUCK. She also wears lavender corduroy pedal pushers, while a streaked flow of silver hair, apparently still wet from a recent shower, falls past her shoulders. "I won't be stupid and ask you what it's about," laughs Jane, sinking the one answer I'd prepared, "but—is that it?" and accurately gestures toward the manilla folder I'd laid, as casually as possible, on the sofa beside me. I nod and in the ensuing pause find myself handing it to her.

She takes it, puts it on her lap, and says:

* * *

Listen. Usually I give the advice: Enjoy the journey. Because the destination is Shit City.

Unless I think you're a contender.

Do you think you're a contender? Don't answer that.

But if I think you're a contender, then I say: If you can, *give up*.

But we both know you can't. Anyway, I have no advice. Please. Who are we kidding. Advice!

I am going to tell you about something I heard a comedian say.

But look at the room, Jane Kim continues. The light is changing. The air is either speckled or pink. You put down the words they go one way or another. You might get it wrong, or, in a rare and lucky moment, you might get it right. And then you weep, not from accomplishment born out of fierce effort, but simply from wonder. And the next time you look, it might not be right after all. That's the game. It's not up to us—though I admit when I was your age I thought fatalists and fools were one and the same.

I won't even touch what happens after that, after the writing, when it gets made into a piece of marzipan or a love-affair simulation. That's just the storm outside the window.

I wish it were different! Just today I was corresponding with A. World. Famous. Writer! Crème de la fucking crème.

As well as, two days ago, A Poor Washout, and just yesterday I spoke with a friend who is Still Toiling in Obscurity. And all these sometimes hold the light.

But even the Successful One lives mostly in the gray fog. Despite the admiring public and the hideaway houses on the coasts. His songs are impeccable. The orchestration isn't maudlin or an exaggeration but the true power of symphony. Yet his nights are occasionally sweaty too. I mean to say to you: *There is no hope if your direction is pure.*

I once saw Allan Havey, a comedian, speak about bombing. Do you watch stand-up comedy, so-called? No? It's marvelous, grotesque. And it *must* be punctuated by laughs, that's the constraint. That's the rule.

And in its art, there is a secret birthplace. Eating it. *Bombing.* The crowd not even against you—just bored, indifferent. *They don't think you're funny.* Nothing lands. You are onstage in a widening ring of silence.

And I heard the comedian say: *So you want to know what bombing is like?*

You have leaped from the plane and are falling.

You have a plan. You have a kind of blinkered faith.

You have a parachute.

It is the anticipated time. You pull the cord. Nothing.
You pull the secondary. Nothing. The instant onslaught of
panic as the sliver of ideation concerning your destruction
begins to grow.

And, the comedian continues, it doesn't end. The bombing.

Onstage, there's the flop sweat and the terrible silence.
The silence is a rose-red scarlet letter smothering you with
what isn't there. If not the silence then the booooos. And you
die onstage and slink off while trying hard not to slink, not
to show the *slink* in the slink and the dying doesn't end, the
bombing the falling the flailing panic the dying doesn't end.

It doesn't end when you come offstage. When you come
offstage: still, you are falling and panicking.

When you grab your coat and say your goodbyes and
leave the venue: still you are unfunny and unloved, still you
are panicking and falling. The heart of the fear of public
speaking. The heart of the fear of disclosure. When driving
home and fighting traffic, still you are falling and panicking
and panicking and falling, unloved, unfunny. When lying
in bed. When waking up. Dying, continuously. The next
day and the next day and the next, over your morning coffee
and when you open your mailbox in the afternoon and when
you dry your dinner dishes. Unloved, unfunny. You have
written the novel of your life and no one will acknowledge
it let alone publish it. Still the spastic reaching that never
arrives, the heart brimming with shame. Unfunny, unloved.

It sounds like *failing*, doesn't it? But it's being born. Falling and falling and falling.

Soon after, we finished our drinks. I don't think it was the booze—more what Jane had said to me. But, in any case, the rest is a blur.

All I can remember is that I found myself, dazed, an automaton, thanking Flora and Jane for their courtesies. I was led to the door. Jane clutched the folder with my manuscript and wrapped an arm around Flora's waist. Empty-handed at last, I stepped away from their door and into the dark.

MY FIONA

by LISA HSIAO CHEN

IT DID ME NO good, but I went to see *Solaris* again.

It's not my favorite Tarkovsky film. That would be *Mirror* or *Stalker*. But it sometimes happens that a work of art chooses you. And so I found myself buying a ticket for the matinee show at the cinema on Houston Street. This was on a Sunday afternoon after a rain. I remember feeling a bit adrift, not unlike, I suppose, Kris Kelvin when we first encounter him in the movie, detached from the world around him as he wanders the grounds of his father's dacha with a wounded air. He might as well be in outer space, and, in fact, that's where he's headed.

When I entered the dimness of the theater, I could see it was nearly empty. The pandemic was not yet over. A couple, their knees pointed toward each other, spoke in low tones in the back. A few cinephiles—older, male, alone—had planted themselves in separate rows. I had a flickering thought, illicit and mildly thrilling, that we were breathing in pestilence for the pleasure of seeing a movie at its intended scale. The nutty odor of popcorn charred the air.

In the dark, I let the familiar story line wash over me. Kris Kelvin, a psychologist, is recruited to investigate the strange happenings aboard a space station circling Solaris, a remote planet. The surface of the planet is mostly ocean, a sentient ocean capable of burrowing into people's minds and materializing, in flesh and blood, "visitors" from their past. This happens to Kris. He wakes up after his first night on the station to find his wife, Hari, who has been dead for some years, gazing at him from across the room. She is aglow, the lambent light from the porthole window illuminating the down on her cheeks.

I found my thoughts drifting to Fiona.

Even if you didn't know her name or have never heard her perform, you'd probably recognize Fiona if you've seen her picture. She's the classical pianist with the waist-length hair and high-slit gowns, the virtuoso in the shimmering micro-dress charging through the score, equal parts thunder, knife, poetry, crushing and caressing the pedals with her signature four-inch Louboutin heels, a C-suite masochist's wet dream. There is that Fiona. But the Fiona I was thinking of was my Fiona, if I could claim such a thing. I was remembering an ordinary morning at her apartment all those years ago when *Solaris* was on my mind, as it was now.

At the time I was her personal assistant, or, as she preferred, her chief of staff. Apart from me, she had an entire entourage on her payroll, including a business manager, a lawyer, a publicist, an accountant, a stylist, a makeup artist, and a personal trainer. But I was her second brain, a predictive algorithm. I handled her complicated travel arrangements, her calendar, and correspondences.

In my experience, people who make a lot of money don't necessarily end up buying more things. Quantity is finite; quality isn't—which is why rich people are exceedingly particular about the things they can't imagine living without. I made sure Fiona's refrigerator was stocked with pressed juices, exquisite triangles of soft French cheese, and oat milk, or whatever variety of milk substitute was currently in vogue. For rice, she required haiga, a specialty grain half milled to remove the bran, leaving the nutrients intact. I learned to prepare her favorite comfort food: Hong Kong–style toast drenched in condensed milk.

It was late morning when I arrived at Fiona's condo on the thirty-third floor. She wasn't at the piano but sprawled on the leather sectional sofa facing the floor-to-ceiling windows and panoramic view of the skyscraper forest. Her thin frame was swallowed in an oversize sweatshirt, her long hair pulled into a ponytail sprouting from the top of her head. She wiggled her fingers at me in greeting, still fixated on her phone. I nodded in return. I took a plate down from a kitchen cupboard and began cutting up the pain aux raisin I'd bought on the way over. I knew she was, in fact, happy to see me, but this performative nonchalance was one of our routines. After months of touring, the departures and arrivals, the forced smiles and good manners, the grasping fans and fawning handlers, Fiona wanted nothing more than to slip back into her life with as little fanfare as possible.

I was, I think, one of her few friends. At least I believe she thought of me as her friend. A beloved mentor lived in Berlin, but the nature of their relationship made true friendship difficult. When once he'd taken it upon himself to endorse her young talent with the weight of his reputation, over time it was she who made sure he still felt important and relevant in his old age. I rarely heard her mention spending time with anyone in her peer group in a context that was not professional. It didn't help that she was on the road for most of the year; when she was home, she practiced ten hours a day. It was often midnight by the time she stopped practicing, too late to call anyone or go out for a bite to eat.

Except there was someone to call: me.

Sometimes she'd ask that I be there at her apartment late at night, so by the time she stopped working, slightly delirious and in a fugue-like state, I'd be ready to join her for a snack or a session of bad television. Her mood often turned on how well she had played that day. One night she might be tired but exhilarated and would be playful with me, turning over the label in my collar and objecting that my pullover was not only from, horrors, the Gap, but *Gap Factory*. (She made grudging allowance for Uniqlo because Asian.) On another night, when she could not master a sequence despite plunging into it repeatedly, she might be petty and mean. Once, when I brought over a to-go container of mac and cheese at her request, she took one bite, leaned over her garbage pail, opened her mouth like a dump truck, and gagged theatrically before screaming at me. There have been times I could have sworn by the way she narrowed her eyes that she wanted to pinch or slap me. She had that common affliction of artists—or anyone, I suppose—at the top of their game: a conviction that their outsize passions and achievements ought to permit them abominations deplorable in others.

Did I enable her solitude? Could I truly be considered her friend when she paid me? I admit I would, on occasion, blur the lines by staying late or arriving early. A friend warned me that I was contributing to my own exploitation, but I didn't see it that way. I used to think this was a character flaw of mine. It turns out people who are very good at one thing are often quite bad at life. This is where I came in.

As I prepared a kettle for tea, I recounted for her a scene from *Solaris*, which I had watched in bed the night before: Kris has arrived on the space station and is meeting one of the onboard cosmonauts, Snaut, for the first time. As they talk, Snaut shows Kris something he's rigged in his private quarters: a row of long strips of paper affixed to some kind of venting system. As air from the vent blows, the paper flutters, an approximation of wind rustling the leaves of a tree.

Night is the best time here, says Snaut, bug-eyed and haggard. It somehow reminds me of Earth.

So what is that you miss about Earth, I asked Fiona, when you touch down from your travels?

She turned away from her phone, amused by my question.

I know this sounds strange, but when I come back to New York, it's the smells I miss. Even the subway smell I miss—that hot metal stink.

But when she went home to see her parents, she said, it was different. There, it wasn't a smell that delivered her sense of belonging but a sound: the cry of the koel.

Her parents, both schoolteachers, still lived in her childhood home on Ap Lei Chau, an island separated from the Hong Kong mainland by a bridge. All her life, they'd supported her talent and her career, even though it had meant long separations from their only child.

The koel is a common bird in Hong Kong, Fiona continued. It's the male koel who has the dramatic looks—he's black, so black he's almost blue, with eyes the color of blood! He's the one with the distinctive song. It's a mating call that signals the start of the monsoon season.

Here, I'll demonstrate. Fiona straightened herself, lifting her chin in the manner of a practiced performer, and cried out, *Coo-eh! Coo-eh!*

All through her childhood, she'd hated that bird. She was preternaturally sensitive to sound: loud noises and certain pitches set her on edge.

It's not a nice bird, Fiona said darkly. They lay their eggs in the nests of other birds. A total hostile takeover. And those red eyes—so cold! They are like a *Terminator* bird. When

I was a girl, I asked my parents for a slingshot so I could pick them off one by one.

Did they give one to you?

No. They're much more Buddhist than I am. Much more kindhearted too. Leave the birds alone, they told me. They are just being birds.

By now I had prepared the tea and pastry, which I arranged on a bamboo tray with a linen napkin and set before her on the coffee table. Fiona appraised the presentation appreciatively, and held her hands out for the cup I poured.

She said when she left home for conservatory, she was happy to leave behind the bird that had cost her so many hours of sleep. But when she returned from school for the first time and heard the koel's plaintive, horny song, she was nearly moved to tears.

She waved me closer and reached for her phone.

See, I made a recording. He's the ringtone for my parents now. Her eyes were soft as she looked at the tiny circle attached to the contact number, a gray-haired couple in brightly colored puffer vests, their heads tilted toward each other to fit inside the perimeter of a selfie. Fiona laughed lightly, which was what she did to deflect too serious a feeling.

I said for me it wasn't a smell or a sound that made me think of Taiwan, but a particular brand of instant noodles.

It was a brand my family favored when I was a child and we still lived in Kaohsiung, with red-and-orange-striped packaging and a jaunty rooster emblem. Sometimes we ate it raw for a snack, sprinkling the contents of the flavor packet over the crisp brick. Like the special sauce slapped onto American fast-food burgers, the proprietary spice blend made the whole meal cohere. After my father died and my mother moved us to Los Angeles to be closer to her older sister, the noodles vanished, like so many other things in our new lives as immigrants. My mother started cutting hair. I started piano lessons. I started cram school. I started doing speed.

And then came the day I found myself seized by a taste memory, the noodles and their implacable capsicum tang. I dove into the internet, assuming, at first, that I'd find them easily. But I could find no evidence of them except in the bowels of an obscure website devoted mostly to Taiwanese politics and pop culture for diasporic readers. Someone in a forum had posted a query about the noodles that they, too, remembered eating in Taiwan, describing the same striped packaging and the rooster. A few others responded with equal yearning, reporting the noodles' disappearance from their local Asian grocery stores. One person said that the noodles had been discontinued by the manufacturer, while another claimed a massive fire at a factory in Taichung had driven the company out of business.

The post that generated the most heat was by someone who insisted that the noodles had been rebranded under a different name. A detractor riposted that they had sampled the facsimile brand and it was a definitive fake, to which the original poster fired back—on the grounds that they had personally eaten the original noodles in question hundreds, if not *thousands* of times—that there was no question the new brand was authentic and that the flavor profile we all remembered so fondly had been faithfully restored.

So how about you? Did you try that other brand? Fiona prodded.

Intoxicated by her pity, I struggled to keep a smile from touching my lips. I shook my head, partly because I doubted it was the real deal, and partly because I'd been waging a flea-sized boycott of the multinational e-commerce site where those noodles were being sold. I soon forgot about the whole thing, I told her, and years passed, and once again I found my tongue tingling, and once again I burrowed online in pursuit of relief. I repeated the same dogged search, revisited the same site, and re-read the full thread, including a few new feckless updates. I discovered an entirely separate forum where someone had begun an identical thread about their failed pursuit of the noodles and read through all the responses on that platform as well. I've started to think, I said to Fiona, that my ritual search through the internet's back alleys, my quasi-annual communion with netizens who share my thwarted ecstasies, has become a consolation for the noodles themselves.

Fiona sighed and rested her head in the crook of my neck.

I'm so sorry for your loss.

No, I'm so sorry for *your* loss, I said.

But I haven't lost anything! She laughed. In the next instant, she jerked up and stuck her lower lip out, an affectation of childlike petulance that I imagined she thought was adorable but I found slightly repugnant.

Is that what's going to happen to me when you're away? I'll have to survive on instant noodles. And wear my dirty clothes over and over again!

I had informed her a month earlier that I would be taking a vacation, my first real one since I'd started working for her. The truth is I found the whole concept of vacations something of a burden. I had no travel companion; I didn't know whom to ask. The thought of promising someone a "fun time" paralyzed me. Short on ideas and then, finally, on time, I ended up hastily booking a bus tour of a region in Scotland that had gained some fame as the location for a television show I'd been watching, despite myself, about time-traveling lovers.

Part of our game, which was not always a game, was that Fiona was the enfant terrible used to getting everything she wanted, while I toadied around her muttering, *Yes, boss*, doing my best impression of Tattoo on *Fantasy Island*, a show I'm not sure Fiona had ever seen but that still made her laugh.

You won't even know I'm gone, I said, pressing my palm against the side of the teapot to test its warmth. I just picked up your laundry a few days ago, and I promise you won't go through even a fraction of your underwear drawer before I get back.

Why should I even wear underwear while you're away? Fiona set her half-drunk tea down with a *thonk*. No one will even notice!

Well, you might as well wear your nasty period ones, then.

A wicked smile flickered across her face. Do you know how many men would pay to get my dirty panties in the mail?

I told her I did, because I was the one who fielded her fan mail. One thoughtful pervert had even included a pre-addressed, stamped envelope.

I told her: What we should do is mass-produce them— buy a stack of cheap underwear from Nordstrom Rack, rub a wedge of Parmesan cheese along the crotch, and stuff them in sandwich bags with dates guaranteeing freshness.

Fiona squealed, covering her mouth with both hands, and pummeled her feet against the arm of the couch. You are disgusting, she cried. Then she yawned broadly like a cat and sank herself farther into the cushions. Without makeup, her eyes appeared guileless. She arched her back and rearranged herself. That was my cue to slide a hand down the front of her joggers.

She made a mewling sound as I deepened my stroke, using my middle finger as a bow. Then I rubbed, jiggled, and zigzagged. I cycled through all the settings of a Hitachi Magic Wand Plus. She writhed a little against me but mostly kept still. I knew she liked the sensation of being held in place while her pussy behaved uncontrollably, so I hooked my leg around hers. She moaned and closed her eyes. I looked her full in the face and proceeded with the greed of a snout. Her eyelids fluttered as she rode the volta of her arousal until she came, and then she opened her eyes as though emerging from a dream, and, like someone who realizes she's been observed while sleeping, looked both bashful and pleased by the attention.

* * *

A few months after this exchange, Fiona fired me. Later I would learn that this was a pattern of hers: one day you were her favorite person, and the next you would find yourself an insect impaled beneath one of her vertiginous heels.

She fired me by text.

I remembered I was emerging from the subway when I read the message. A stranger, annoyed that I had slowed my pace up the stairs, charged past me and banged my elbow. My heartbeat thundered in my ears. I was stung, yes, but more so, I felt hot with shame, as though I'd done something unforgivable. But what had I done? I tore through my memory banks, frantic as Pacino in *Dog Day Afternoon*. She never gave a reason. She wrote that I should know why. A cruelty, this final thumb in the wound.

That was years ago. For a while I was a personal chef for an older couple, an emeritus music professor and her banker husband. When they moved into assisted living, I cooked for a wealthy family whose neuroses manifested as food allergies so baroque I was obliged to make individualized meals for each person. I found no real joy in this work. More recently, I started my own boutique catering outfit specializing in Asian fusion small bites. Even now, when I speak with a prospective client, Fiona inevitably comes up. I describe how I met Fiona's expectations of excellence in matters great and small, and how I'll bring this discerning competence to bear on their own event and whatever bloated sense of importance they assign to it.

What was Fiona like? people want to know. I can't blame them for their curiosity. I try not to give a rote answer. I use each occasion to draw out some facet of her being from my recollections. It's not unlike when you've seen a film multiple times, to the point where you're no longer immersed in narrative and are free to train your attention on specific aspects of its making.

At this matinee screening of *Solaris* on Houston Street, I chose to focus on the soundtrack.

The story is Tarkovsky didn't want a soundtrack at all but someone to orchestrate the sounds of nature, he said, according to the laws of music. The composer Eduard Artemyev complied by producing a churning, oneiric score that made use of an arcane instrument known as the ANS synthesizer. Picture a cross between a mid-century supercomputer and an IKEA PAX wardrobe unit. It was the brainchild of Yevgeny Murzin, a Red Army audio engineer whose dream was to convert images—visually drawn sound waves—into sound.

Fiona was the only person I knew who'd seen the ANS synthesizer in real life. (Was that why my mind that day at the matinee had tuned in to the soundtrack? Or had the music made me think of Fiona?) The only one that still exists is displayed at a music museum in Moscow. Years ago, before she met me, Fiona was scheduled to perform in that city. In her downtime, she visited the Glinka Museum, which goes by a different name now. This was in late March, still wintry in Russia. After taking full advantage of her hotel's sauna and gym, she went on a brisk walk to the museum. (I imagined her hair still slightly damp, stuffed under a fluffy Cossack hat.)

As she made her way through the museum galleries, she stopped before a room lit by stained-glass windows. A tall man with a gray mustache stood speaking in front of what looked like Frankenstein's jukebox. It was the ANS synthesizer. Curious, she slipped into a chair in the back row. The room was under-heated, as were most buildings in that country. She thrust her hands beneath her thighs to keep them warm. The lecture was in Russian, but she gathered that the large glass sheets that fronted the instrument were the surface on which one etched patterns and shapes, which were then fed through a mainframe that somehow converted these squiggles into tones, or music.

I remember I asked Fiona what the synthesizer sounded like. She closed her eyes. These types of questions she handled, always, with seriousness and care.

Like a lonely whale who is lost in an ocean made of steel and glass, she said.

The tragedy of *Solaris* is that the visitors seem so real. They can be touched, although, uncannily, their skin is as soft as a newborn's. Their voices sound just as we remember. But there's a catch—this is science fiction, after all. The visitors don't have selves beyond our own memories of them. Visitor Hari is horrified by this, a crisis that leads her to kill herself by drinking liquid oxygen. Or does she kill herself because that's how Kris remembers her, as suicidal? The visitors are monsters. We, along with the ocean, are their Frankenstein.

When the credits began rolling, I leaped to my feet. I was the first one out the door. The theater had begun to stultify; for the first time I could remember, I had become bored with the world inside the film. It was a relief to exit the building and feel the cold air scrape against my skin.

Of course it has occurred to me, then and now, to reach out to Fiona, to attempt to repair whatever it was that had been broken. The overture would be awkward, but I don't think she'd resist. And then what? We'd make a plan to have sushi or coffee. As the date approached, she'd cancel but reschedule, and we'd manage to meet, two and a half months later. After that, it would be another seven or eight months, and after that, well, we'd probably be where we are now.

I wanted the impossible: to pick up where we'd left off in the long conversation of our lives. Did she know, for instance, that the ANS synthesizer was used at some point by the Russian military to communicate with dolphins? The idea was to train them to plant mines and protect naval bases from enemy divers. Last week I read that dozens of dead dolphins have washed up on the shores of the Black Sea. Scientists think it has something to do with the war in Ukraine, that the proliferation of sonar from warships and submarines is scrambling the dolphins' echolocation. They're crashing against rocks they can't sense, Fiona, they're starving to death, unable to track their prey.

THE INSTEADMAN
by KEVIN HYDE

THE RICH COUPLE ARE down at the club. They're almost always down at the club, where they golf among the birches and pines and discuss the state of the day, the fine quiddities of it, and tax laws with their fellow members, the staff, and the caddies. The rich couple are in the midst of a spirited round against an old retired couple whose fitness and health they find mysterious and a little grotesque. They're a few strokes ahead when the man remembers they've scheduled a dinner party for that evening with a few of the town's bigwigs, the mayor and mayoress, the postmaster, and one of the area's notable lawnsmen. He curses the heavens and throws down his putter in frustration just as his wife is about to putt, causing her to miss her birdie. But they confer after she finishes and agree that they cannot abandon the round, not when they're so close to beating the old retired couple, who stand on the other side of the green, exuding wholesomeness in their radiatingly white orthopedic golf spikes, and a kind of odd, challenging athleticism that always seems to state wordlessly that their sex life is better and more vigorous than the rich couple's, a vibe that the rich couple find infuriating. The gardener, they remember, is still on duty and could serve as a host pro tempore for the dinner party. The rich man races back to the clubhouse in their golf cart and yells at an attendant, "Get my gardener on the horn!" While waiting for the attendant to return with the phone, the rich man imagines the possibilities established by this precedent, if it comes off: The gardener as his proxy. An unpleasant office meeting? The gardener. A boring chamber of commerce gathering? The gardener. A long-delayed dentist visit? The gardener. What is the difference, after all, between one man and another? Isn't it only by the blind lottery of birth that each man is who he is? Mightn't the rich man be the metaphorical gardener for someone richer and more powerful than he is? Just then, the attendant brings the phone and the rich man shakes his head to empty it of these thoughts. He gives the gardener instructions to serve whatever comes out of the oven, even if the cook burns everything black. "Be a friend and hold down the fort for a little while, would you?" the rich man says. When the rich couple return home, after being soundly beaten and taunted by the old retired couple, they find the dinner party in full flow, bottles of champagne and liquor everywhere, the gardener regaling the guests with an anecdote about how he recently took a bath in the commodities market. Everyone laughs but the rich man, who will trace the origin of his later heart trouble and decline back to this moment, when the charming gardener unseated him from his place in the world.

TWO FLOORS ABOVE
THE BUTCHER

by AMIT CHAUDHURI

I STOPPED LISTENING TO Neil Diamond around 1977. I was drawn to him when I was eleven or twelve, in '73 or '74, and he became part of my weekly listening routine, along with a bunch of other musicians, some of whom I became disloyal to very quickly (like the Carpenters and John Denver), and others whom I continued to flaunt till I was sixteen (like the Who, Deep Purple, the Beatles, Paul Simon). Neil Diamond inhabited a location between these extremities. I had only two records by him: *Hot August Night*, the capacious double-album recording of a live performance at the exotic Greek Theatre in Los Angeles, and his *Greatest Hits.* Of the tracks on the latter, "Cracklin' Rosie" and "Sweet Caroline" were too optimistic and upbeat for me, but there were other songs I listened to even when I no longer owned up to doing so:

"Holly Holy," "Brother Love's Travelling Salvation Show," "Brooklyn Roads." I liked the way Neil Diamond could work up raucous emotion (as in "Holly Holy") with, predominantly, two chords and words that didn't mean very much ("Holly holy eyes"). The way Diamond created energy and affirmation with just a couple—or barely more than a couple—of major chords (the simplest of harmonic structures) in songs like "Cherry, Cherry" and "Holly Holy" makes me think of him, retrospectively, in relation to the African musicians who created the "happy tunes" that became important to Paul Simon. This affirmation seemed part of his makeup, but it was also vulnerable to a commercialization that turned it into something cheerful—with songs like "Sweet Caroline," to an extent, but more so as his career progressed and the world itself, with the onset of the '80s, changed to a marketplace.

"Brother Love's Travelling Salvation Show" was so full of voices, personae, and shifting imagery that listening to it felt like watching a short film; with its portrayal of the ecstasies of evangelism one "hot August night" inside a "ragged tent" in the South, it was evidence of Diamond's gift for delving into local histories that lay well outside his Jewish childhood in Brooklyn. Sitting in my drawing room in Malabar Hill in Bombay, I had as diffuse an idea of what "gospel" and "preaching" meant as a boy in Manhattan or London would have had, but songs like Diamond's (besides comic books and movies) gave those diffuse sensations the immediacy of the local—they felt more real, sometimes, than my actual surroundings. The drawing room in Bombay seemed pallid at

times. To escape it, I went to my uncle's house in Calcutta—
or to the urgent realities encountered in such songs.

The song I liked best on *Greatest Hits* was "Brooklyn
Roads." No one who listened to Neil Diamond ever mentioned it. I wonder now how it made it onto the *Greatest Hits*:
Was it an indulgence on Diamond's part? Nor have I been
able to track down a live recording except a middle-aged
version which I've not had the courage to listen to in its
entirety. The way the song lay concealed within the album—
there but not there, camouflaged as a hit and thereby doubly
unnoticed, taken to be a hit but never spoken of—meant that
the relationship I had with it was equally hidden, part of my
pop-song landscape but also outside it. Though I couldn't
make out every word, I could follow most of them—enough
to realize that something deep was being recovered in the
song, deep and deeply ordinary, things that didn't find a
place in pop songs:

> When I close my eyes
> I can almost hear my mother
> calling, "Neil, go find your brother..."

The first shock was the word "Neil." The names of pop
stars were indistinguishable to me from inventions, and,
to a thirteen-year-old who still didn't know Jewish names
well, "Neil Diamond" was generic, like "Ziggy Stardust" or
"David Bowie." It was disorienting and affecting to regis-
ter, each time I heard the song, the singer singing his own

name and reliving his mother's voice and directive. Why was I affected? I had no brother myself. My mother was in the midst of life. I didn't need to "close my eyes" to see her. The act of recall in relation to her and my home would come eight years later, when I'd go to London. The "closing of my eyes" would come after 2016, when she died. But a part of me already contained who I would become, which included what I would lose, just as the person I would become would contain who I had been (which contained who I would be). That same echoing space-time was also the experience of the man who had written the song.

Dinnertime made up the song's opening scene:

Go find your brother.
Daddy's home and it's time for supper.
Hurry on.

Having closed his eyes to bring back the past, Diamond gazes upon it as if it were happening to someone else, and the lyrics shift to the third person:

Two boys
racing up two flights of staircase,
squirming into Papa's embrace
and his whiskers warm on their face.

Then there's a groaning return to the present: "Oh, where's it gone?," which would risk sentimentality were the song mourning a greater loss, but is made real by its longing for the banal. The chorus locates the childhood precisely:

> Two floors above the butcher,
> first door on the right,
> and life filled to the brim
> as I stood by my window
> and I looked out on those
> Brooklyn Roads.

I took this to be a provincial location, slightly cut-off but "filled to the brim" with its own reality. The songwriter I met in "I Am... I Said" seemed to be a kind of universal voice laying claim to a city that existed only in the popular imagination:

> Well, I'm New York City born and raised,
> but nowadays I'm lost between two shores.
> LA's fine but it ain't home.
> New York's home, but it ain't mine no more.

This was the kind of thing any songwriter could say, irrespective of nationality. New York in pop songs (like Elton John's "Mona Lisas and Mad Hatters") was the place everyone belonged to and had been exiled from. "Brooklyn," in Diamond's song, was inalienable and non-metropolitan; I forgot, listening to the song, that it was in New York.

The next bit of "Brooklyn Roads," still lingering on

"smells of cooking in the hallways," moves closer to the kind of boy I was becoming by the time I was fourteen: "report cards I was always afraid to show." Then there were my parents' visits to school in 1976: "Teacher'd say he's just not tryin.' / Got a good head if he'd apply it." In bringing back that conversation, Diamond revisits some of the upheaval it caused. The boy's way of coping was familiar:

> I built me a castle
> with dragons and kings,
> and I'd ride off with them
> as I stood by my window
> and looked out on those
> Brooklyn Roads.

By the song's end, the singer speculates on a form of continuance:

> Does some other young boy
> come home to my room?
> Does he dream what I did
> as he stands by my window
> and looks out on those
> Brooklyn Roads?

The life that Diamond describes was more like my cousins' lives in Calcutta—two brothers and a sister; flights of stairs in a three-story house; smells of boiling rice, mustard oil, talcum powder—than my hovering, incorporeal existence in a twelfth-story apartment in Bombay, looking out not from a window onto a street and other windows, as my cousins did, but—where California and Manhattan merged—on the expanse of the Arabian Sea, the palm-fronded Marine Drive, and the tall buildings of the '70s skyline. Desiring other worlds ("dreaming") gave me corporeality: I led a plausible, proxy childhood in Calcutta, and Diamond's Brooklyn felt close for those three minutes, as if I were racing up the staircase myself. But through the shifts between selves that poetry and fiction create, and that make ideas like point of view and identification limited in their usefulness, I was also that "other young boy" who came "home to my room." The contradictions language accommodates without blinking! How could another person come "home" to *my* room? It was possible, apparently. You become part of someone's life without knowing it.

In 1977, I began to direct my attention to Joni Mitchell. The next year I started learning North Indian classical music. I became less up front about having listened to Neil Diamond.

In September 2022, almost exactly three years after I'd last been there, I was in New York again, accompanied by my wife, having strategized for the dates of my visit to coincide with the publication of a novel. We stayed on Second Avenue in Manhattan, not far from the United Nations—though we never ventured in that direction, but walked only toward Third Avenue and Grand Central Terminal. I had loved New York's "terrible oxygen" of fumes and urine when I'd visited it in 1979. It had seemed incomparably novel, like Calcutta. (The words I've just put in quotation marks are from Elizabeth Bishop's "The Fish." They're meant to remind us that an environment that's life-giving for one creature [man] may be fatal for another—the fish of the title. In 1979, New York was proof that the opposite was also true: a noxious atmosphere can be vitalizing.) By the time I went to New York again, in 2000, something in it had died, and what I experienced on subsequent visits was a hollowness. But on this occasion (Was it my wife's company? Had something in New York come back to life after the pandemic? Or both?), I was more grounded and felt connected to the city's everyday—like the lonesome people who ambled outside the homeless shelter on Forty-Fifth Street—in a way I hadn't before.

So, in that upbeat mood, I started making plans for expeditions: not just to the Met or MoMA or Central Park or the High Line, but to revisit with my wife half-remembered locations from my pre-pandemic excursions in the city—places I didn't really know but where I'd crossed a street or arrived at a junction or church and thought, There are parts of this city that are real, after all, or where I'd stored away a number, like Thirteenth Street. I did not know exactly where to go, but clung to the realization that there was more to New York than I'd assumed. Ever since we'd passed through

Chelsea in an Uber one afternoon (a September afternoon in which one neighborhood gave way to another like cards fanning out) on the way to a venue (the City Winery) at which I was going to perform, I'd thought we should return later to look for the Chelsea Hotel. This was because of these lines, which contain something epochal and unfinished:

> I remember you well at the Chelsea Hotel.
> You were talking so brave and so sweet.
> Giving me head on the unmade bed,
> while the limousines wait in the street.

Unfinished because the act itself seems incomplete, unless it comes to some sort of fruition later; there is also that moving, clumsy shift to the present tense in the fourth line, as if the singer is distracted by the possibility that the limousines are *still* waiting. This was a song that had not been in my Leonard Cohen selection (*Songs of Love and Hate*, et cetera) as a teenager. I discovered it on YouTube seven or eight years ago. It immediately brought back the world of that time as well as the fact that much of it was unknown to me. And my wife and I did find the hotel two afternoons post–Uber ride. I have always eschewed author-related tourism. If I should come upon a poet's house, living or dead, by accident, or because someone has taken me there by the scruff of my neck, all well and good. But as an objective in itself, it never seems worthwhile. But pursuing the scent of songs! That's a different matter. It was on this trip that the fact that songs can be habitations crept up on me. I wanted to know what the Chelsea Hotel was. Expectedly, it's a tourist destination. We viewed it from outside—so recognizable, like a building on Chowringhee—and then went in for ten minutes, barely noticed by the doorman. We peered into the bar and used the bathroom, as we always do when we're at a hotel. Within and around it, the atmosphere was sexually charged, a large part of the charge emanating from a tall androgynous woman who dominated the corridor and who, when we walked out, was chatting with the doorman. This was the kind of area that took a step further the pink-rimmed spectacles and pink shoes that have multiplied in the last decade; a home for every common-or-garden exhibitionist. When your gaze fell on them, as mine did on a muscular man who had adorned his bare torso with a dinner jacket and bow tie, they looked deflated, as if I'd brought back a memory of a place they'd come from and were pretending no longer existed. My wife and I did not belong here. Still, we liked Chelsea very much.

Then my wife left. She was scheduled to fly back a week before me. I had to deliver a lecture in Massachusetts and perform in a concert. Then I would return to New York for a day and a half, though that drawing out of my stay served no clear purpose. I wanted to go home. But suppose something came up beyond my planned itinerary, something I hadn't foreseen when finalizing my schedule? The last day and a half were added for such a possibility.

An author I hadn't seen for years and I decided to have lunch on the day of my departure. On the penultimate day, I thought I'd follow up on a long-deferred project: interviewing the poet Charles Bernstein with my phone camera at MoMA, where he'd elaborate on what he'd called, when my wife and I had visited MoMA in February 2019, "MoMA's view of modern art." Ever since that evening, I had hoped to one day record Charles's—not his *tirade*, but the part-flippant, part-interrogatory stream of thought he'd shared with us as we'd walked through the various rooms. I'd had to wait three years—and for the pandemic to recede—to record this conversation. We decided to meet at MoMA at 11:00 a.m., before the crowds entered in full force.

But for more than a week, I'd been thinking of "Brooklyn Roads." I had been thinking, on and off, of Neil Diamond. As I walked between gigantic outgrowths of buildings, snatches of lines came back to me: "Neil, go find your brother"; "it's time for supper. Hurry up." I'd already been to Brooklyn on this visit, to Greenpoint Avenue, an area that still retained accumulations of history—the everyday of another time—in its facades. But the boutiques were there, too, disguised but unmistakable. Across an empty lot, you could see the East River. Still, the area had a purity that I had missed in DUMBO, my first experience of Brooklyn, in 2013. When I'd taught at Columbia University for a term in 2002, a friend, Merv Rothstein, had urged me to go to Brooklyn, where he'd grown up, to check out the museum. The semester ended and I realized I never went. A decade had passed, but DUMBO was not what I had expected Brooklyn to be. This was because DUMBO itself, caught between gentrification and the ghosts of old neighborhoods, didn't know what it was.

I googled "neil diamond's birthplace" and "neil diamond house brooklyn"; I googled "Brooklyn Roads." I discovered he'd lived in the Coney Island section of Brooklyn. From comic books, Coney Island had associations for me of fairground violence: bright lights, Ferris Wheels, gangs. Yet Wikimapia gave exact coordinates for "Neil Diamond's childhood apartment" as Church Avenue, N 40°39'3", W 73°56'54"—or perhaps these numbers located what were classified as "related objects": Tövhid Mescidi (with the *e* facing the opposite direction) and Ram's Roti Shop. A box that said "apartment building" above it, but displayed only a gray strip running through a light gray background, had the caption, "The Apartment Neil Diamond sang about in Brooklyn Roads is on the third floor of this building. These are the windows he 'looked out on those Brooklyn Roads.'" Custom NYC Tours had a post from 2017 whose opening sentence was promising: "I was contacted by someone today about the possibility of doing a Neil Diamond–themed tour in Brooklyn." Another post from four years ago by the same man—Jeremy Wilcox, who claimed he often walked by Diamond's old apartment—revealed that a one-off excursion had taken place but evidently had never been repeated. I began to feel frustrated, but also very close to the communities, individuals, and shadow-objects I encountered on these pages. I also found that Diamond had grown up in a house near the Oceana Theater, a movie hall by the Brighton Beach subway stop.

Post-MoMA, after I'd had lunch and said goodbye to Charles Bernstein, I realized I had nothing to do for the rest of the day. I weighed my options and decided to go to Brighton Beach. I had no idea where or what it was. I liked the name.

Google Maps said it would take me an hour to get there. This would mean two hours spent on travel and maybe an hour or more looking for Neil Diamond's house. This was a bigger commitment than any I'd made so far in New York. I had avoided parties and social calls on this visit— almost everything except promotional trips. Thinking these thoughts, I made my way to Grand Central Terminal from Fifth Avenue.

A self from another historical age wondered if I would get lost if I went that far. My present self reassured me that that wasn't possible; I had a smartphone. What I had to do was make sure I didn't lose my iPhone (which I had done in New York in 2019, in a taxi)—but I was more careful these days about the trousers I wore and the pockets they had.

At the entrance to Grand Central, a few seconds in, someone always sat next to a shop on the floor, with their feet stretched out, reading aloud to themselves from a book, ignoring passersby and being ignored. This was the last familiar thing I'd see for a while. I took the line 7 train to Times Square, not sure if it was uptown or downtown I wanted, and then I took the line Q to Coney Island, three stops before which was Brighton Beach. There was also the line B, whose last stop in the Brooklyn direction was Brighton Beach, which I didn't take for some reason.

Once I was aimed at Coney Island, I relaxed and allowed myself to puzzle over which stop I really wanted. The previous day, I'd seen a video, posted twelve years ago, of Neil Diamond arriving on Church Avenue with the intention of walking to his erstwhile "home." In fact, the video was called "Welcome Home Neil Diamond." It was mobile phone footage; he had caught the attention of passersby because he had a camera crew with him. Maybe they were making a documentary. The first question he got was from a Black woman, clearly curious about his entourage: "What's your name?"— an ingenuous and, under the circumstances, engaged query, and Diamond sees it as one; he smiles and shrugs slightly and says, "Neil Diamond." "Ah, okay, Neil. I'm Angie," says the woman. "Hi, Angie!" says Neil, and then, in reply to another question, "I lived here when I grew up here when I was a kid." "You gotta be kidding! How many years ago?" "You want me to tell you for real?" "Yeah." "Fifty." "Fifty *years?* I've lived here since... thirty... thirty-seven years. Guess how old I am." Now comes a display of Diamond's gallantry: "You look like twenty-one to me." "Oh, thank you! I'm forty-eight." "*No...*" In that moment the video is no longer about Diamond but about Angie and how exceptional she is. It is about her life story, emerging from Diamond's life story ("I lived here when I grew up here"), which she knows nothing about. And I felt it was possibly the same for me; that I had a life outside my own on Church Avenue. Diamond himself looks middle-class, not in the English sense of being university-educated, but of being modest, unassuming, on the right side of the law, a man who did not disappoint his parents. In a sense, he's free of his tortured pop past, free to wander Church Avenue. He points to the front and says what sounds like "I grew up here, between Argo and Westminster Road." I don't know if "Argo" is right. I google it. I wonder if I should disembark at Church Avenue.

But I didn't. I went to Brighton Beach in the state of arrest that comprised the protracted journey. The train wasn't full. It was also not stopping at each stop on the line. People got on and off without the fixity of purpose you saw in central Manhattan. As we went farther, the commuters grew visibly desultory and more remote from whatever it is that drives Manhattan and the rest of the world. I asked a girl with vaguely punk-like attributes if I was on the right train and she nodded with the pity and understanding you show a stranger, and confirmed, when she got off, how many stops away I was. To emerge into sunlight again was a revelation: bits of the city I had not seen before and didn't know when I'd see again. I subdued my restiveness, my urge to get off at Church Avenue, for example, or Cortelyou Road, which research had told me was germane to my quest. As the train

moved closer to my destination, I took photos of some stations because of their vacancy and width and pastoral names
(Sheepshead Bay), but the pictures couldn't capture what
I saw. As we pulled into the Brighton Beach station, the
tracks seemed to narrow, shielded by platform, and from the
window I saw rooftops, flat and white, platform-level, ripple
back, a counter to the infinitely high buildings I'd been with
on my visit and the memory of which had started receding.

Everything here was narrow, staircases and escalators
included. I didn't know in which direction to exit, and, as is
often the case in the United States, but was especially true
here, a porter and I spoke to each other in English without
understanding each other, as if each were speaking a foreign
language. When I descended and walked under the frozen fil-
igree of steel girders and then crossed the road in the sunlight,
I obeyed Google Maps and turned left. Out of the corner of
my eye, or with eyes I had in the back of my head, I spotted
a shop called Tashkent Supermarket under the bridge. From
the journey so far, and the view from the platform, I knew—
as if I had already lived here for a month or more—that this
was a predominantly Russian area. But the war with Ukraine
seemed as removed from what I was entering (as I walked
farther in) as Manhattan did: this was a Russia of groceries
and retired people. At the end of the brief stretch I saw two
street signs, CONEY ISLAND AVENUE and VALERIY 'LARRY'
SAVINKIN STREET, the first reiterating that I was deliciously
close to the edge of nowhere, the second reminding me how
street signs are at once local and universal; they make you

intimate with a history even if you have no idea where you are, something you forget when you're surrounded by names that perform their own meaning, like Columbus Circle, and tell you, literally, that you've "arrived." Discovery stops there.

I crossed the road after those signs. My destination was at hand, Google said. A woman was rearranging things in her shopping bag and, next to her, on a bench on the pavement, a man who could have been from anywhere was speaking and swearing into his mobile phone in a severely Punjabi-inflected Urdu. SHOE REPAIR, read a shop sign, with presumably the same words below in Russian. An elderly lady in a red cardigan was reviewing her display of porcelain dolls and crockery on a table. Behind her was the New Brighton Jewish Center. I realized I was on the wrong side of the road. I asked a woman (almost everyone had shopping bags with them; maybe not being at home meant holding shopping bags) if she knew where Neil Diamond's house was, and she said, "Who?" Guarded by scaffolding were a couple of optimistic figures: a small man with a rucksack, and a woman who was wearing what appeared to be a combination of a Rajasthani ghaghra and a costume for a Bollywood dance number, complete with head covering, goldwork, and border. They seemed like neither migrants nor tourists, but something out of Picasso. I didn't bother to ask them about Neil Diamond. Instead, I said: "Where are you from?" The woman said, "Russia," and I asked if I could take a picture.

A taxi company came up. By now I knew that the Oceana Theater, the continuous warehouse-like block next to me, had been converted into a supermarket. "Did Neil Diamond live here?" I asked the operator behind the glass. I spelled the name and asked him to look it up on the internet. "Ah, a singer!" He assessed me, not without empathy. He said the Oceana Theater was where we were. We were both talking about a man and a location that one of us thought he knew and the other thought he didn't, but neither could be sure that what he knew was, in fact, true. Having wasted each other's time, we parted cordially. I stepped into the sunlight, turned at the end of the road, went up the steps, and peered inside at stacks of fruit. I confirmed that the supermarket also occupied the second floor. I had in mind some corroboration of the precise directions: "Two floors above the butcher, first door on the right." Whatever might have corresponded to this had been replaced by something that wasn't simply a usurper but had its own ongoing heaviness and presence. Or it was likely that I hadn't got my bearings right.

Crossing the road, I entered a park that had curving art deco steps going up to areas where retired men and women sat on benches, waiting for a moment when, as at the end of a film, they'd reach the end of what they'd come for. As is always the case, the men looked indifferent and at ease and the women subtly unhappy. I felt the urge to sit on a bench and become part of the park's life, but something in me, a posthumousness, resisted and drew back. One is so often at a threshold of another life but chooses to retain, in a moment of wakefulness, what one takes to be one's identity. So I turned back toward the metro station, thinking, But where is Brighton Beach? Is there such a place? A Sikh appeared, white-bearded, in a purple salwar kameez, and I followed him, as you do a person who reminds you of home, in case they *take* you home. But he did not, and instead stopped at a shop on the boulevard, going in and, with equal efficiency, coming out in a few seconds because they didn't have what he wanted. I took a photo of him against the light—a diffuse, blinding radiance surrounding him, as if there had been an explosion. He noted me without caring, as ghosts or beings not bound by gravity hardly care for the living, among whom he counted me. I would always remember seeing him, as you do a being from another world, but I would have no place in his memory. The light behind him indicated (I didn't think this then; I feel it now) that the sea was *that* way, which is probably why I kept walking, turning at Brighton Sixth Street, stopping to peruse the Soviet delicacies on the menu of Café Euroasia, going farther, ostensibly to embrace the buildings, but also because I had glimpsed the ocean. I finally came to the boardwalk. Frozen largesse: gold—the sea, sand, and sunlight. It made me feel Brighton Beach was a fiefdom unto itself. A young woman in a bikini, every part of her body reflecting the sun, was complaining to an old man, her companion: "It's hard, you know? It's not easy." He was like the aging hunger that sought nourishment; she like the prize that telltale marks say is not as young as it seems. Next moment, after I'd veered off and returned, they were like brother and sister reunited, he a prematurely aging boy, she shrinking into childhood, curled up against each other on the deck chair.

I went back to the stairs going up to the metro station and had to decide how to proceed. The Oceana Theater location might have been wishful thinking. I could go back to Manhattan; that would be a relief. I mustn't tire myself out before a long journey—although the journey back to India the next day felt long only academically, in light of my present outing. I could check out Church Avenue, where Diamond had been when he'd said he was heading for the place he'd grown up in. What was the name? Westminster Road. To get there, I'd need to get off at Church Avenue, or at Cortelyou Road and take a bus. Where on Westminster Road, though, was this apartment, "two floors above the butcher"? I got onto a line Q train headed toward Manhattan, putting in abeyance the stop where I'd eventually get off. I disembarked at Newkirk Plaza. Its platform tapered to a point where only two human beings could stand comfortably. (Consulting my photo, I see this is not strictly true. The entire platform is narrow and tapered, and the end feels like a jetty, like an idea that's fading, because you can see the tracks vanish from there.) There was an object on the platform that was neither palanquin nor cage. It was latticed on top and had a gazebo-type covering. It was locked. At first, I thought there was an animal inside. It could be that metro employees traditionally kept their belongings in it. I waited for the train to Church Avenue.

Church Avenue underlined what the video had suggested: it was in a Black (and, as I'd see, Jamaican) district. Even to cross at a traffic light was a tropical event. I asked a couple of people about Westminster Road, and they complied with a wishful "over there," as if saying so might make it true. So I decided to go down East Eighteenth Street instead.

Turning left into Albemarle Road, I found a group of women, between fifty and sixty years old, chatting in front of an old residential building. They were so absorbed and happy and oblivious that I wanted to introduce myself. "I have a question," I said. They blinked, as at an incursion by a fly or a ball from across the street. "Any idea where I might find Neil Diamond's house? I've heard it's in these parts." "Neil who?" In a moment, this changed. One of them said, "Oh, the singer! I know who you mean!" They looked a bit put out. "Oh, he's in Manhattan!" This threw me. "In Manhattan?" "Yes, Manhattan!" It came to me that she was conjecturing that anyone successful must live on that side of the city. "No, no, the house in which he grew up! Haven't you heard it's in Brooklyn? Have you heard 'Brooklyn Roads'?" This put them into a semi-embarrassed state of recouping. "Where you from? India?" I was impressed by how I embodied my nationality so transparently. "Yes!" "You just got here, fresh off the boat?" Boat? I reached for a word with which I have never described myself, except at an airport immigration desk: "No, no, I'm a tourist! I'm going back tomorrow!" "Oh, a *tourist*." Those were rare here.

I thought I'd proceed toward Ocean Avenue—the light, which I assumed was from the ocean, made hazy what felt like a terminal bit of the city: pure surface, one-dimensional, inscribed with letters and graffiti. A young man on a motorcycle was coming up the pavement, moving, in a double infraction, in the opposite direction from the cars on the street. Then he swerved gently into a building entrance. This momentary turbulence hinted at something topsy-turvy—a contrary flow. What I saw farther off, where Albemarle Road ended, wasn't Ocean Avenue, in fact; Ocean Avenue was yet another crossing. What I was approaching—a city wall—was beyond it, the closeness an optical illusion. Then I grew distracted by the Salem Missionary Baptist Church, the structure itself futuristic, as someone might have once conceived of the future. Having read up a bit more on the building, I find it was built in 1958 as a synagogue, and then merged with the Baptist Mission in the '70s. The truth is that things are ever-changing; that's what I must have felt, passing, already prepared for this departure from fixity by the counter-directional motorcycle on the pavement, and the end (Ocean Avenue) which gave way. The real border turned out to be Flatbush Avenue, the wall the (scaffolding-veiled) facade and sign of the Assembly Hall of Jehovah's Witnesses.

There was a lot of God about. On the way back to Church Avenue, I took a small detour off Albemarle Road to investigate the Flatbush Seventh-day Adventist Church. Back again on the capacious avenue, I overheard a group of loiterers, men and women, murmuring in French. West Africans. I had a feeling that these people—who viewed questions to do with street directions or Neil Diamond with suspicion—would open up more readily about God if asked. This is just an inkling, but I've noticed that working-class people, including those I've overheard in Calcutta, have a special investment, a greater sense of excitement in discussing God, or gods, or even life and destiny, than they do loans, property, or sports, but not because of a desire for paradise or salvation: it's as if the discourse liberates them for a while from the terms they've been presented with to measure themselves: livelihood, small attainments, expectations, duties. Having paid nothing for it at all, they want to inhabit the overarching long term, of life itself, but also, in India, of birth and rebirth, and not just the time of deadlines and the finite day.

On my way back, too, a motorcycle boarded the pavement, disregarding the boundary between route, thoroughfare, and home.

On the other side of Albemarle Road, I noticed a "white person." She was walking a dog. A "white person" is a euphemism for an outsider. The word *white*, in its associations with "outsideness" (outside communities, outside culpability), represents a reversal of terminology. In this reversal, the outsider controls the world.

I'm not an outsider, despite claiming a tourist identity (over and above my Indian one) to the women I was talking to. I find the places I recognize are my own, intimately.

* * *

From evening, bridge, and sky, we entered a tunnel at some point, and remained ensconced going to Times Square. I understand this now: that to resist gentrification, Brooklyn must move away from the East River. Any glimpse of the East River allows, at that point, global markets a way in.

Also, home. It's a cliché to say so, but one must choose between home and elsewhere. We have chosen elsewhere. This journey back to Manhattan is also a journey away from home; not Neil Diamond's home, but something, some world, we repeatedly leave behind.

There are no easy solutions to knowing where to go. Tomorrow, when I fly back to India, I'll be choosing elsewhere again. I'll have the vaguest memory of where I started.

LILLE ALLEN is a Latinx designer and writer based in Las Vegas. Currently the in-house designer at *Eater*, Lille was the associate art director at the *Believer.* Her writing can be found on *Hyperallergic* and on little pieces of trash across America.

BIANCA BAGNARELLI is an Italian cartoonist and illustrator. She is the cofounder of Delebile, an independent label publishing comics by young Italian and international authors. Her first comics volume, *Fish*, published by Nobrow, won the gold medal for the short form at the Society of Illustrators in New York. She has worked as an illustrator for the *New Yorker*, the *New York Times*, the *Atlantic*, *National Geographic*, Penguin Random House, *La revue dessinée*, among other publishers and publications.

AMIT CHAUDHURI is a novelist, essayist, and musician. His eighth novel, *Sojourn*, was published by New York Review Books last year. His album, *Across the Universe*, will be released this year, when New York Review Books will also publish his *New and Selected Poems*.

LISA HSIAO CHEN is the author of *Activities of Daily Living* and *Mouth*. Her writing has appeared most recently in the *Baffler* and the *Brooklyn Rail*. She was born in Taipei, Taiwan, and now lives in Brooklyn, New York.

PATRICK COTTRELL is the author of *Sorry to Disrupt the Peace*. He teaches at the University of Denver.

VÉRONIQUE DARWIN writes and teaches in the ski town of Rossland, British Columbia.

TOVE DITLEVSEN was born in 1917 in a working-class neighborhood in Copenhagen. Her first volume of poetry was published when she was in her early twenties and was followed by many more books, including the three volumes of the Copenhagen Trilogy: *Childhood* (1967), *Youth* (1967), and *Dependency* (1971). She died in 1976.

OLIVIA GALLO was born in 1995 in Buenos Aires, Argentina. She is the author of the short-story collection *Las chicas no lloran* and a collection of pandemic correspondence with Tamara Talesnik called *Intranquilas y venenosas*. She has run a creative writing workshop since 2021.

EDWARD GAUVIN has volunteered for Red Cross disaster relief, led middle school wilderness expeditions, taught English at various domestic and foreign colleges, stocked tires in a warehouse, editorially assisted with the in-house monthly glossy of a professional association for executives of other professional associations, and distributed brochures for a British tour service to hotels in the Somme. From this history it may be possible to estimate his momentum, although doing so will preclude any determination of his whereabouts.

FRANCISCO GONZÁLEZ is a Wallace Stegner Fellow at Stanford University. His fiction appears in *Arts & Letters*,

Gulf Coast, the *Southern Review*, *Zyzzyva*, *The Best Short Stories 2022: The O. Henry Prize Winners*, and elsewhere. He holds an MFA from Columbia University.

SHARI GULLO founded the Big Ugly Book Drive, which sent more than fifty-four thousand books to residents in the "book deserts" of West Virginia's coal-mining regions. Shari's now working to install Illinois's tallest peace pole in Lake Zurich, where she lives. Her hero is Dr. Martin Luther King Jr.

KEVIN HYDE's work has appeared in *Ninth Letter*, *Redivider*, *Gigantic*, *McSweeney's Internet Tendency*, *Asymptote*, *Parcel*, *Big Fiction*, and elsewhere. He received his MFA from the University of Florida. He lives with his wife and two kids in Tacoma, Washington.

MORTEZA KHAKSHOOR was born in 1984 in Iran. He has exhibited his work widely in the United States and internationally since 2011. Solo exhibitions include *The Quiet Path to Otherwhere* (online) at Taymour Grahne Projects in London (2023); *Stubbly Numbness* at Emma Gray HQ in Santa Monica, California (2022); *Dirty Words and a Melody* at Wilder Gallery, London (2022); and *Forty-One Drawings and Prints 2016–18* at California State University Art Gallery in Turlock (2018). He is the recipient of many awards, including the inaugural Emerging Artist Award at the Editions/Artists' Book Fair in 2018. His works are in private and public collections, most notably at the Ford Foundation Center for Social Justice in New York. He currently lives and works in London.

E. TAMMY KIM is a contributing writer at the *New Yorker* and a cohost of the *Time to Say Goodbye* podcast.

JULIA KORNBERG is a writer from Buenos Aires, Argentina, living in New York. She is the author of the novel *Atomizado Berlín*.

EUGENE LIM is the author of the novels *Fog & Car*, *The Strangers*, *Dear Cyborgs*, and *Search History*. He works as a high school librarian, runs Ellipsis Press, and lives in Queens, New York.

KIT MAUDE is a literary translator based in Buenos Aires, Argentina. He has translated dozens of writers from Spain and Latin America for a wide variety of publishers, publications, and institutions, and writes reviews and literary criticism for publications in Argentina, the United States, and the United Kingdom.

DREW MILLARD is a writer from North Carolina who lives in Philadelphia. His first book, *How Golf Can Save Your Life*, is due out in May 2023 from Abrams Books.

ANUJ SHRESTHA is an illustrator and cartoonist residing in Philadelphia. Clients include the *New York Times*, the *New*

Yorker, the *Washington Post*, *ProPublica*, *Wired*, and *Playboy*. He is fond of chili sauce, horror movies, and chihuahuas.

MAYA SOLOVEJ is a translator and writer from Copenhagen, Denmark. Her work has appeared in the *Baffler*, *Astra*, and the *Brooklyn Rail*, among other publications.

SPARROW lives in a double-wide trailer in the prudish town of Phoenicia, New York. His latest book is *stories* (Apathy Press). Sparrow's favorite rapper is Rod Wave.

RYAN THOMPSON is an artist and educator from Chicago. He likes thinking about how people come to believe the things they do about their place in the natural world. See more of his work at www.departmentofnaturalhistory.com.

SARAH WANG has written for the *London Review of Books*, the *Nation*, and *n+1*. She is a PEN America Writing for Justice Fellow, a Tin House Scholar, a Center for Fiction Emerging Writer Fellow, and a Sewanee Writers' Conference Tennessee Williams Scholar. She teaches at Barnard College.

THE SPLENDID TICKET
by Bill Cotter

Angie Bigelow has hit the jackpot: a $324 million lottery ticket. How will she spend the money? Will she share it with the father of her children, dissolute Dean Lee Grandet—even though he's an inveterate gambler she plans on leaving? With a fast-moving plot, packed with originality and heart, this is the story of the Grandets discovering the alchemy that holds their family together, testing its limits, and running headlong into whatever their futures hold.

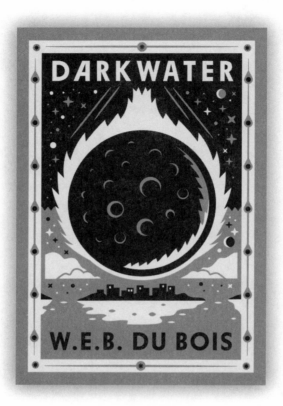

DARKWATER
by W. E. B. Du Bois

In *Darkwater: Voices from within the Veil*, early twentieth-century statesman of discourse W. E. B. Du Bois weaves autofiction with poetry, social essay, science fiction, and Afrofuturist storytelling in a work that presages Octavia E. Butler, Tananarive Due, Nana Kwame Adjei-Brenyah, Nisi Shawl, and N. K. Jemisin. Du Bois plunges readers into his multifarious and mysterious text, one that begs us to examine how Black American experiences have changed these last hundred years—and how they remain the same.

GRIEFSTRIKE!
THE ULTIMATE GUIDE TO MOURNING
by Jason Roeder

When it comes to grief, there's no room for second-best. Sure, there are other guidebooks aimed at helping you cope with the emotional and practical challenges of losing a loved one. None, however, have been written by a comedy writer whose "therapeutic training" went no further than an undergraduate degree in psychology, and who lived through this terrible experience and emerged intact enough to write a bunch of jokes about it.

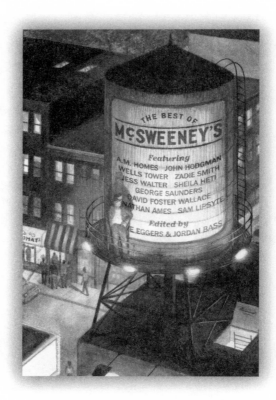

THE BEST OF McSWEENEY'S
edited by Dave Eggers and Jordan Bass

To commemorate the fifteenth anniversary of the journal called "a key barometer of the literary climate" by the *New York Times* and thrice honored with a National Magazine Award for fiction, here is *The Best of McSweeney's*—a comprehensive collection of the most remarkable work from a remarkable magazine. Drawing on the full range of the journal thus far, *The Best of McSweeney's* is an essential retrospective of recent literary history, and lasting proof that the contemporary short story is as vital as ever.

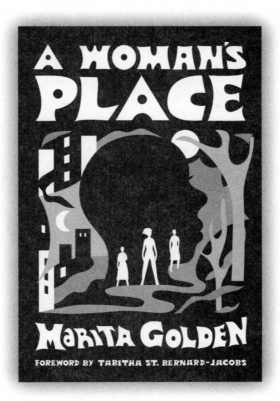

A WOMAN'S PLACE
by Marita Golden

It is 1968 and everything about being a Black woman in America is changing. Three young women meet at a New England college and form a friendship that endures, heals, and dramatically shapes their lives. Faith, Crystal, and Serena each struggle to determine a path for themselves as they navigate expectations set by race, gender, and their families. Originally published in 1986, *A Woman's Place* is reprinted here with a new introduction by the author and a foreword by Women's March cofounder Tabitha St. Bernard-Jacobs.

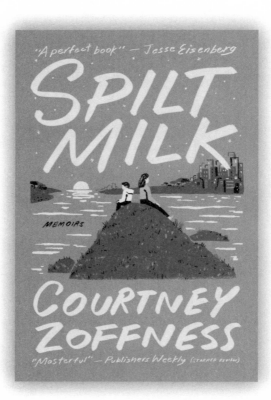

SPILT MILK
by Courtney Zoffness

What role does a mother play in raising thoughtful, generous children? In her literary debut, Courtney Zoffness considers what we inherit from generations past—biologically, culturally, spiritually— and what we pass on to our children. Zoffness relives her childhood anxiety disorder as she witnesses it manifest in her firstborn; endures brazen sexual advances by a student in her class; grapples with the implications of her young son's cop obsession; and challenges her Jewish faith. These powerful, dynamic essays herald a vital new voice.

ALSO AVAILABLE
FROM McSWEENEY'S

FICTION

HUMOR

COLLINS LIBRARY

ALL THIS AND MORE AT

STORE.MCSWEENEYS.NET

Founded in 1998, McSweeney's is an independent publisher based in San Francisco. McSweeney's exists to champion ambitious and inspired new writing, and to challenge conventional expectations about where it's found, how it looks, and who participates. We're here to discover things we love, help them find their most resplendent form, and place them into the hands of curious, engaged readers.

THERE ARE SEVERAL WAYS TO SUPPORT MCSWEENEY'S:

Support Us on Patreon
visit *www.patreon.com/mcsweeneysinternettendency*

Subscribe & Shop
visit *store.mcsweeneys.net*

Volunteer & Intern
email *contact@mcsweeneys.net*

Sponsor Books & *Quarterlies*
email *amanda@mcsweeneys.net*

To learn more, please visit *www.mcsweeneys.net/donate*
or contact Executive Director Amanda Uhle at
amanda@mcsweeneys.net or 415.642.5609.

McSweeney's Literary Arts Fund is a nonprofit organization as described by IRS 501(c)(3). Your support is invaluable to us.